Cambridge Elements

Elements in the Philosophy of Immanuel Kant
edited by
Desmond Hogan
Princeton University
Howard Williams
University of Cardiff
Allen Wood
Indiana University

THE MORAL FOUNDATION OF RIGHT

Paul Guyer
Brown University (emeritus)
University of Pennsylvania (emeritus)

Shaftesbury Road, Cambridge CB2 8EA, United Kingdom

One Liberty Plaza, 20th Floor, New York, NY 10006, USA

477 Williamstown Road, Port Melbourne, VIC 3207, Australia

314–321, 3rd Floor, Plot 3, Splendor Forum, Jasola District Centre, New Delhi – 110025, India

103 Penang Road, #05–06/07, Visioncrest Commercial, Singapore 238467

Cambridge University Press is part of Cambridge University Press & Assessment, a department of the University of Cambridge.

We share the University's mission to contribute to society through the pursuit of education, learning and research at the highest international levels of excellence.

www.cambridge.org
Information on this title: www.cambridge.org/9781009464468

DOI: 10.1017/9781009464505

© Paul Guyer 2024

This publication is in copyright. Subject to statutory exception and to the provisions of relevant collective licensing agreements, no reproduction of any part may take place without the written permission of Cambridge University Press & Assessment.

When citing this work, please include a reference to the DOI 10.1017/9781009464505

First published 2024

A catalogue record for this publication is available from the British Library

ISBN 978-1-009-46446-8 Hardback
ISBN 978-1-009-46449-9 Paperback
ISSN 2397-9461 (online)
ISSN 2514-3824 (print)

Cambridge University Press & Assessment has no responsibility for the persistence or accuracy of URLs for external or third-party internet websites referred to in this publication and does not guarantee that any content on such websites is, or will remain, accurate or appropriate.

The Moral Foundation of Right

Elements in the Philosophy of Immanuel Kant

DOI: 10.1017/9781009464505
First published online: December 2024

Paul Guyer
Brown University (emeritus)
University of Pennsylvania (emeritus)
Author for correspondence: Paul Guyer, paul_guyer@brown.edu

Abstract: Kant defined "Right" (*Recht*) as the condition that obtains among a population of physically embodied persons capable of setting their own ends who live on a finite surface and therefore cannot avoid interaction with each other if each is as free to set their own ends as is consistent with the freedom of all to do the same. He regarded this rational idea, heir to the traditional idea of "natural Right," as the test of the legitimacy of the laws of any actual state, or "positive Right." He clearly considered Right to be part of morality as a whole, namely the coercively enforceable part, as contrasted to Ethics, which is the non-coercively enforceable part of morality. Some have questioned whether Right is part of morality, but this Element shows how Kant's "Universal Principle of Right" follows straightforwardly from the foundational idea of Kant's moral philosophy as a whole.

Keywords: Freedom, right, humanity, the state, Kant

© Paul Guyer 2024

ISBNs: 9781009464468 (HB), 9781009464499 (PB), 9781009464505 (OC)
ISSNs: 2397-9461 (online), 2514-3824 (print)

Contents

1 Is Kant's Doctrine of Right Part of His Moral Philosophy? 1

2 Kant's Definitions of Right 6

3 Freedom, Morality, and Right: Kant's Core Argument 13

4 Political Morality 39

   List of Abbreviations 58

   References 59

A constitution providing for the **greatest human freedom** according to laws that permit **the freedom of each to exist together with that of others** (not one providing for the greatest happiness, since that would follow of itself) is at least a necessary idea, which one must make the ground not merely of the primary plan of a state's constitution but of all of the laws too. (CPR, A 316/B 373)[1]

1 Is Kant's Doctrine of Right Part of His Moral Philosophy?

In the Western tradition there have been two basic justifications for the existence of the state as a form of social organization with the right to use coercion to control the behavior of its members. On the one hand, there is the idea that acceptance of rule by a state is recommended by prudence, and should be governed by considerations of prudence, whether that is the prudence of the governed, as Thomas Hobbes assumed in his argument that the state should be like a powerful Leviathan in order to prevent conflict among its subjects, or the prudence of those who govern, what they need to do in order to hold on to their power, as Niccolò Machiavelli advised princes. On the other hand, there is the view that submission to the rule of law is part of the moral obligation – and therefore corresponding right – of human beings, however moral obligation is understood, whether as divinely commanded, as in John Locke, or not. Immanuel Kant clearly thought of submission to the rule of a state as part of morality, which for him is grounded not in divine command but in the nature of reason itself, fully accessible to human beings with their own resources. The goal of prudence is happiness, but Kant is emphatic that providing for the happiness of its members is *not* the proper object of the state, and any thought otherwise can only lead to what he despises as "paternalism" (TP, 8:290). Since for Kant all practical reasoning reduces to either prudence or morality, if the necessity of submission to the rule of a state is not grounded solely in prudence then it can be grounded only in morality.[2] This is why Kant's first published presentation of his political philosophy, the section "On the Relation of Theory to Practice in the Right of a State" in his 1793 essay "On the Common Saying: That May Be Correct in Theory but It Is of No Use in Practice," is subtitled

---

[1] The list of abbreviations for Kant's works precedes the References. Passages from the *Critique of Pure Reason* are cited by the pagination of its first ("A") and second ("B") editions; all passages from other Kant's works by volume and page numbers from Kant (1900–). Translations are generally from the volumes of the Cambridge Edition of Kant cited in the Bibliography, which reproduce these forms of pagination. In citations from Kant, boldface reproduces his emphasis, in *Fettdruck* in the original text, italics his use of Roman type for what he regarded as foreign words, and the occasional underlining for my added emphasis. In my own text, italics are used for emphasis.

[2] On Kant's exclusive and exhaustive contrast between prudence and morality, see, among many others, Gregor (1963, pp. 35–6); Mulholland (1990, pp. 2–3); and Ripstein (2009, pp. 3–5).

nothing other than "Against Hobbes" (TP, 8:289).[3] The project for this Element is to demonstrate that Kant's political philosophy is indeed grounded in his moral philosophy.

Kant addressed political philosophy chiefly in three texts published in the 1790s, namely, the 1793 essay "Theory and Practice" just mentioned, the pamphlet in the form of a mock treaty *Toward Perpetual Peace* (1795), and the first half of his treatise on *The Metaphysics of Morals* (*Metaphysik der Sitten*) of 1797, namely, the *Metaphysical Foundations of the Doctrine of Right* (*Metaphysische Anfangsgründe der Rechstlehre*). The *Rechtslehre* or *Doctrine of Right*, as it is usually called in English, was published in January of 1797, followed in August by the companion *Metaphysical Foundations of the Doctrine of Virtue* (*Metaphysische Anfangsgründe der Tugendlehre*). The two parts were published together as a single book later that year although the Introduction to the book as a whole had already been published with its first part, followed in 1798 by a second edition with an Appendix of replies to one of the first reviews of the *Doctrine of Right*. Kant had previously lectured on the topic of *Naturrecht*, or "natural right," using as his textbook the *Ius Naturae* (*Law of Nature*)[4] by the Göttingen professor of philosophy and law Gottfried Achenwall, a dozen times, for the last time in 1788 (or maybe 1790); one set of student notes from the offering of that course in the summer semester of 1784 is known, which has been published under the title *Naturrecht Feyerabend*, named after the student who took or at least owned the notes.[5] In addition to these student notes, many notes in Kant's own hand, apparently made in preparation for drafting the *Doctrine of Right*, also survived, at least until World War II, and these have also been published. These are the materials that we have for interpreting Kant's political philosophy.

Kant himself did not call his doctrine of Right "political philosophy."[6] As we will see, Kant himself did speak of "politics" (*Politik*) and "politicians" (*Politiker*) in an important Appendix in *Towards Perpetual Peace*, in which he distinguishes between "moral politicians," who take "the principles of

---

[3] On Kant's attitude toward Hobbes, see Williams (2003) and Guyer (2012).
[4] This work was originally published as *Elementa Iuris Naturae* by Achenwall and Johann Stephan Pütter in 1750. Achenwall took over sole authorship with the third edition of 1763, which was what Kant used. Achenwall and Pütter 1995 is a Latin-German edition of the original work, and Achenwall (2020a) and (2020b) are English translations of Achenwall's solo editions.
[5] The *Naturrecht Feyerabend* was originally published in Kant (1900–), edited by Gerhard Lehmann, in volume 27.2.2 (1978), pp. 1317–94, and in a much more accurate version, edited by Heinrich P. Delfosse, Norbert Hinske, and Gianluca Sadun Bordoni, in Kant (2010–14). Frederick Rauscher's translation in Kant (2016) is based on the latter.
[6] I will use the italicized name "*Doctrine of Right*" to refer to Kant's text from 1797, and the nonitalicized phrase "doctrine of Right" to refer to the contents of this and the other texts mentioned. I explain the capitalization of "Right" in what follows and in Section 2.

political prudence in such a way that they can coexist with morals [*mit der Moral*]," and mere "political moralists," who frame their "morals to suit the statesman's advantage" (TPP, 8:372). But he never referred to his doctrine of Right as political philosophy, and perhaps we should not either. For by "a right" Kant meant an obligation that morally could and should be coercively enforced, and by "Right" he meant the totality of such appropriately coercively enforceable rights. In Kant's view the principles of Right should ground both the legitimacy and the limits of politics, but politics – and therefore political philosophy – concerns the implementation of Right in real-life circumstances, and may also include social goals at the subnational, national, and supranational levels that go beyond what we might think of as properly coercively enforced. So what we mean by politics and political philosophy may be broader than what Kant means by Right. Kant always uses the permissibility and necessity of coercive enforcement as the criterion of what belongs in the domain of Right,[7] and therefore construes the doctrine of Right more narrowly than we might now conceive of political philosophy, although as its indispensable foundation.

But if not as "politics" and "political philosophy," then how should we translate Kant's terms *Recht* and *Rechtslehre*? After all, we – speakers of contemporary English – are familiar with the use of "right" as an adjective, meaning correct or appropriate from any number of normative standpoints, whether scientific, mathematical, aesthetic, social, moral, or political, as well as with the use of "a right" to refer to a particular moral or political entitlement, but we do not use "right" in the singular to refer to the totality of coercively enforceable obligations, and Kant's usage of "right" in that way – *Recht* – can seem strange to us. So people have sought other translations of Kant's term. Some have tried "law," since we do associate coercive enforcement with "law" in its juridical sense.[8] But Kant has another word for "law," namely, *Gesetz*, and it would only cause confusion to translate both *Recht* and *Gesetz* by "law," especially since Kant, like anyone else, assumes that there are laws in force in any actual state that are *not* right or properly part of *Recht*. (For Kant there also laws of nature, for example Newton's laws of motion, that have nothing to do with human conduct, let alone with the coercive enforcement of norms of human conduct; but this is true in ordinary English as well, and is not a source of confusion.) "Justice" has also been suggested as a translation of

---

[7] See Guyer (2016b) and (forthcoming).
[8] For example, the first English translation of Kant's text was entitled *The Philosophy of Law* (Hastie 1887, cited at Mulholland 1990, p. xvi), and Günter Zöller proposes "(juridical) law" in Zöller (2020, pp. 40, 42–3).

Recht; thus, Kant's *Rechtslehre* has been translated as "Doctrine of Justice."[9] But by "justice" we may mean more than what may properly be enforced by human juridical and penal institutions, thus when we call someone "just" we may mean more than just that he abides by codified and enforceable laws,[10] and some people are happy to speak of divine justice. Further, while we might think that justice includes equity, such as paying a servant more than originally agreed to if there has been significant inflation since the agreement was made, Kant argues that this is not an enforceable obligation and thus is not part of *Recht* (DR, Introduction, Appendix I, 6:234–5). Since neither "law" nor "justice" will work, there seems to be no alternative to translating *Recht* as "right." However, to forestall one possible source of confusion, when *Recht* refers collectively to the totality of coercively enforceable obligations rather than to any particular coercively enforceable obligation, that is, *a* right, it will be capitalized as "Right." Thus, the topic of this Element is the moral basis of Right.

This terminological issue out of the way, we can now turn to our central question: Is Right a proper part of morality for Kant? Or does it have some form of normativity distinct from that of morality? Is there some reason other than morality why we should conform our politics to the principles of Right? The definition of "moral politicians" from *Towards Perpetual Peace* says only that for such politicians the principles of political prudence must be able to *coexist* with morals, which could be true as long as one thinks that morality is a supreme or overriding norm, to which any other norms of conduct, whether from aesthetics, etiquette, or politics, must be subordinated, but it does not actually say that Right is *part* of morality. Nevertheless, the answer to this question should be obvious. After all, Kant's *Doctrine of Right* is the first part of his larger *Metaphysics of Morals*, so how could Right *not* be part of morality? Moreover, all of Kant's modern predecessors had thought of Right as part of morality, namely, the coercively enforceable part of morality, that is, the part of morality that morality itself says can and should be coercively enforced if and when that is necessary[11] – and while Kant typically makes it

---

[9] Thus the distinguished Kant scholar John Ladd, who taught at Brown University a generation before I did, translated Kant's *Metaphysische Anfangsgründe der Rechtslehre* as "Metaphysical Elements of Justice"; see Kant (1999).

[10] See Pufendorf (2003, Book I, chapter II, section XII, p. 49). Samuel Pufendorf's *Whole Duty of Man*, first published in 1672 (Pufendorf 2003 reproduces its first English translation from 1691) was a foundational text for both moral and political theory throughout the eighteenth century in both Germany and Britain.

[11] In Pufendorf, for example, all human duties may be divided into duties to God, to self, and to others, and while the first two classes of duty are subject to enforcement by God, only the last is subject to enforcement by human agencies; for example, Pufendorf (2003, Book I, chapter III, section XIII, pp. 59–60). In Achenwall, as in many others, there is a distinction between "perfect" obligations and laws and imperfect ones that is the distinction between coercively

clear to us when he thinks that he is making a significant innovation in the history of philosophy, he offers no suggestion that he is departing from tradition in this regard. However, several distinguished recent commentators have argued that on Kant's account Right is *not* a straightforward part of morality, or is "independent" from it – thus their view is called the "independence" thesis about Kant's doctrine of Right.[12] I think that this independence thesis is false, and that for Kant Right *is* obviously part of morality, namely, the coercively enforceable part of it. I also think, pardon the pun, that Kant was right about this, that is, that we should think of the underlying principles of law and politics as part of morality in general, but here I will attempt to prove only that this is what Kant believed.

Right must be part of morality for Kant given his conception of the foundation of morality itself. This is that the freedom of human beings to set their own ends is the fundamental value that is to be *preserved* and *promoted* in all of morality (see G, 4:430), and that Right is at bottom the requirement that in their actions in pursuit of their own ends – "their external use of their power of choice" in Kant's language – people should leave others as free to set and pursue their own ends as they are themselves, that is, *preserve* freedom for all. Right is simply that part of morality that governs those of our actions that could potentially interfere with the freedom of others. It is certainly not the whole of morality, for it does not include *promoting* freedom in the form of developing our own abilities or assisting others in the pursuit of their own ends, but it is an indispensable part of it, the framework for the preservation of the freedom of all involved in our interactions with each other.[13] After I have laid out Kant's basic idea, I will argue that several points in Kant's political philosophy more broadly understood – his accounts of our duty to leave the

---

enforceable obligations and noncoercively enforceable ones, but always within the class of moral obligations: "A *natural obligation* that, if it is violated, is connected to another man's moral ability to coerce the violater is called a PERFECT OBLIGATION; so an IMPERFECT OBLIGATION is one that is not linked to such a natural right to violence, i.e., that cannot be enforced (exacted by force)"; Achenwall (2020a, §34, p. 13). For more examples, see Guyer (forthcoming).

[12] Leading proponents of the "independence" thesis have included Thomas Pogge (Pogge 2002), Marcus Willaschek (Willaschek 1997, 2002, and 2009), and Allen Wood (2008 and 2014). I have criticized their arguments in Guyer (2002) and (2016b); other important criticisms are Nance (2012), Baiasu (2016), and Pauer-Studer (2016). Here I will focus on my version of the alternative, "dependence" view. Herman (2021, p. 102n42), incorrectly places me on the side of the "independence" theorists.

[13] My approach will thus be closest to those of Gregor (1963), Mulholland (1990), Ripstein (2009), and Pauer-Studer (2016), but I will point out some differences in due course. In saying that Right is indispensable for the realization of morality, however, I do not mean that it is any function of the state, which secures the condition of Right, to itself otherwise actively promote morality (see also Rossi 2005, pp. 63–4).

state of nature and enter into the civil condition, of the duties of rulers, and of the duties of citizens – make sense only on the assumption that for Kant Right is part of morality, not just a matter of prudence.

2 Kant's Definitions of Right

Kant's terminology can be confusing, so let's start with some definitions. We can begin with Right. Borrowing one of his favorite distinctions, we can distinguish between his formal and material definitions of Right, or, using other terms, between nominal and real definitions. The formal definition of Right distinguishes it from what Kant calls Ethics in a narrow sense – the capitalization here will distinguish this narrow sense from the broader sense in which Kant sometimes uses "ethics" (*Ethik*), and in which everyone uses it now, in which it is simply equivalent to morals or morality as a whole. The material definition makes explicit the substance or specific content of Right on which, as it turns out, the formal and/or nominal definition of Right is ultimately based. This formal and/or nominal definition amplifies the one already used in the previous section. This was that Right is the sum of our coercively enforceable obligations, more precisely the sum of the types of our coercively enforceable obligations, or even better the sum of the conditions of possibility of our coercively enforceable obligations. Kant's own statements of this definition make explicit that Right is the sum of the types of our coercively enforceable *moral* obligations, thus define Right as part of morality. Only a part of our moral obligation to others is appropriate for coercive enforcement by others, namely, that part that prohibits limiting their freedom of action more than we limit our own. Ethics, conversely, is that part of morality that cannot be coercively enforced, in the dual sense that it is not possible to coercively enforce the setting of ends and ultimate motivation with which Ethics, but not Right, is concerned, and also that no one has the moral standing to enforce ethical requirements on anyone else. Kant explicates the formal and/or nominal distinction between Right and Ethics as the coercively and noncoercively enforceable parts of morals as a whole in the Introduction to the *Metaphysics of Morals*.[14]

---

[14] This is in what was numbered as Section III of the Introduction in the editions published in Kant's lifetime and in Kant (1900–), but renumbered as Section IV in Bernd Ludwig's 1986 edition of the *Rechtslehre* (Kant 1986), and following him in Mary Gregor's 1996 translation in Kant (1996a) and in John Ladd's second edition of his translation (Kant 1999). Ludwig reorganized the text at a number of points based on the premise that Kant's printer had received a faulty fair copy and that Kant had not, or not carefully, read the proofs. This is clearly right for several passages but controversial for others, including Ludwig's rearrangement of the four sections of the Introduction to the whole *Metaphysics of Morals*. But it makes no difference in what follows whether the material about to be cited is regarded as Section III or Section IV.

Kant begins by stating that

> In all lawgiving [*Gesetzgebung*] (whether it prescribes internal or external actions, and whether it prescribes them *a priori* by reason alone or by the choice of another) there are two elements: **first**, a **law** [*Gesetz*] which represents the action that ought to be done **objectively** as necessary, i.e., which makes the action a duty; and **second**, an **incentive** [*Triebfeder*], which **subjectively** connects a ground for determining the power of choice [*Willkühr*][15] to this action with the representation of the law; hence the second element is this: that the law makes the duty into the incentive. By the first the action is represented as a duty, which is a merely theoretical cognition of the possible determination of the power of choice, i.e., of practical rules; through the second the obligation to act is combined in the subject with a determining ground of the power of choice in general. (MMI, 6:218)

In any case of "lawgiving" there are two elements, one the law that is the content of the lawgiving and the other the incentive or motivation for acting in accordance with the law. Thus there might be more than one possible incentive for complying with one and the same law: "All lawgiving can therefore be distinguished with respect to the incentive (even if it agrees with another kind with respect to the action that it makes a duty)." Kant then exploits this possibility. On the one hand, as indeed he had already anticipated with his remark that "the second element" is "that the law makes the duty into the incentive," "That lawgiving which makes an action a duty and also makes this duty the incentive is **ethical** [*ethisch*]," but on the other hand "that lawgiving which does not include the incentive of duty in the law and so admits an incentive other than the idea of duty itself is **juridical** [*juridisch*]." In case the incentive for compliance with the law need *not* be duty itself, that is, respect for duty or for the moral law that underlies all duty, Kant continues, "the incentive must be drawn from **pathological** determining grounds for the power of choice," that is, not sick or aberrant ones ("pathological" in the contemporary sense), but simply from the domain of "inclinations and aversions" (*Neigungen und Abneigungen*), because on Kant's psychology, or "anthropology" as he calls it, there *are* only two possible ultimate sources of motivation, pure reason on the one hand, which produces both moral law and respect for it as a motivation, and the inclinations and aversions of our sensible nature on the other. Kant then takes the further step of insisting that in the case of nonethical, that is, juridical lawgiving, the incentive must actually be "aversions; for it should be a lawgiving, which constrains, not an allurement, which invites" (6:218–19). In other words, in Ethics, our incentive must be respect for duty or the moral law itself, but in the case of juridical obligation – the domain of Right – our incentive can be aversion, that is,

---

[15] Gregor typically translates *Willkühr* as "choice," which can suggest a particular act of choice or choosing; but for Kant, *Willkühr* connotes the faculty or ability to choose rather than an individual act of choosing, so I will always translate it as "power of choice."

fear of punishment – in other words, coercion. As far as Right is concerned, our incentive for complying with the law can simply be our desire to avoid punishment. Thus we do not offer people rewards for complying with the law,[16] but we do threaten them with punishment for not complying with the law – and of course a threat is hollow and ineffective if we do not carry through with it when there is a violation. The content of Right is those of our moral obligations that are coercibly enforceable – although of course it is possible, and would be nice, that is to say ethical, if people did not sometimes need the threat of sanction to act in accordance with the duties of Right and always did so just from respect for the idea of duty itself. But people are not always motivated by respect for the moral law, thus, although Kant does not make this explicit, in order to make sure that the moral law is nevertheless obeyed, those parts of it compliance with which *can* be motivated by aversive incentives *should* be.

But in either case, the source of obligation – the first element of "lawgiving" – is the moral law and only the moral law – or should be, if the legislation of any actual state, "positive law," is to conform to the "natural law," or Right. Juridical obligation – that is, the *content* of moral obligation, the conduct that it requires – does not have a separate source from the moral law itself, which is also the source of ethical obligation. Kant makes this clear throughout the Introduction to the *Metaphysics of Morals*: "**Obligation [*Verbindlichkeit*]** is the necessity of a free action under a categorical imperative of reason" (MMI, 6:222) – but, as Kant had argued in the *Groundwork for the Metaphysics of Morals*, *there is only one categorical imperative*. The "mere concept of a categorical imperative," Kant had argued there, "also provides the formula containing the proposition which alone can be a categorical imperative," and if the categorical imperative is to be derived from the very concept of a categorical imperative, there can only be one: "There is therefore, only a single categorical imperative and it is this: **act only in accordance with that maxim through which you can at the same time will that it become a universal law**" (G, 4:420–1). Kant repeats this claim in the Introduction to the *Metaphysics of Morals*, with the explicit acknowledgment that it is the sole source of obligation: "The categorical imperative, which as such only affirms what obligation is, is: act upon a maxim which can at the same time hold as a universal law" (MMI, 6:225).

Two points about these statements will be crucial in what follows. (i) The requirement to act only on maxims that could also be universal laws is only Kant's first statement of the categorical imperative in the *Groundwork*. Kant quickly follows it with another version, to act as if the maxim of your action were to become by your will a "universal law of nature," but these two versions are

---

[16] See Kersting (2004, p. 47).

equivalent, for a law that is universal in a world would be a law of nature in it, and Kant treats these two versions as equivalent in his own count of three main formulations of the categorical imperative (G, 4:436). But a second, genuinely distinct formulation of the categorical imperative will be fundamental to the argument of the Doctrine of Right, indeed of the whole *Metaphysics of Morals*: the requirement that we always treat humanity as an end and never merely as a means (G, 4:429). (ii) The first formulation of the categorical imperative says only that one must always *act* only in accordance with universalizable maxims, that is, maxims that can also be universal laws and can be willed as such; neither says that your *motive* or *incentive* must always be this very requirement itself. The categorical imperative itself says nothing about what the incentive for acting in accordance with it must be. The categorical imperative requires just that you *act* only on universalizable maxims, that is, principles of action, or that you always *treat* humanity as an end in itself, never merely as a means. The demand to act out of respect for the moral law and not merely in accordance with it is the condition for what Kant calls "moral worth," *but it is not part of the categorical imperative itself.* For some kinds of duties, respect for the moral law may be the only available incentive for compliance with the categorical imperative, but outward compliance with the requirements of some kinds of duty can be secured by the threat of sanction – in other words, coercion. The cases where the threat of sanction is also available, and indeed where morality itself demands that we put in place a system of sanctions to ensure that people comply with the demands of morality, comprise the content of Right.

The main argument of this Element is that the status of humanity as an end in itself, where humanity is our freedom to set our own ends, is the foundation of Right as well as Ethics, and we will come back to it soon enough. For now we can focus on the second point, which is presupposed by Kant's claims that all obligation stems from the categorical imperative, but there can nevertheless be different incentives for complying with it, namely, the ethical incentive of respect for duty itself and the juridical incentive of fear of coercion. Continuing the passage from the Introduction to the *Metaphysics of Morals* that was quoted at the beginning of this section, Kant adds that "The mere conformity of an action with law, irrespective of the incentive to it, is called its **legality** [***Legalität***] (lawfulness); that conformity, however, in which the idea of duty from the law is at the same time the incentive of the action is its **morality** [***Moralität***] (morality [*Sittlichkeit*])" (6:219). "Legality" is what the categorical imperative itself requires, and all that it requires: action in compliance with the specific duties generated by the categorical imperative in the specific conditions of human existence.[17] "Morality," action not only in accord with duty

---

[17] All that some commentators mean when they say that the duties of Right cannot be "derived" from the categorical imperative is that these duties arise only when the imperative is applied in the specific conditions of human existence, that we are spatially embodied creatures who can

but also "out of" duty, or of respect for duty as its incentive, is a further matter, a requirement for what Kant calls in the *Groundwork* "moral worth" (G, 4:398), worthiness of "esteem."[18] Kant may confuse us by using *Moralität* as the name for this additional factor of moral worth, where we have to translate that Latinate word the same way that we translate the Germanic term *Sittlichkeit*.[19] Although not here, by the latter term Kant usually means all of the requirements of what *we* call "morality," what he often also calls *die Moral* or *die Sitten*, and thus we might understand his distinction between "legality" and "morality" to suggest that those duties that can be satisfied with mere "legality" must lie outside of what *we* call morality altogether. But that is not what Kant means. For him, the *Moralität* of an action refers to the special quality of its motivation, that is, that it is done with the morally worthy motivation of respect for the idea of duty itself. But morality as a whole, what Kant calls *die Moral* or *die Sitten*, specifies the whole range of our moral obligations, those that can and may be satisfied from fear of sanction as well as those that can be satisfied only from respect for the idea of duty. The very title of Kant's book, *Die Metaphysik der Sitten*, is properly translated as "Metaphysics of Morals" and not "Metaphysics of Morality" in Kant's special sense of *Moralität*, because it concerns all of the kinds of obligations that arise from the categorical imperative for human beings, regardless of the incentive out of or by means of

---

interact with each other on a finite surface, in particular who can come into conflict with each other over occupation of the same piece of land. This condition is what Arthur Ripstein calls a "postulate" that must be added to the categorical imperative to generate the duties of Right, thus Right is a "legitimate extension" of but not a "derivation" from the categorical imperative (Ripstein 2009, Appendix, pp. 355–88, especially pp. 361–2, 370–2). Kant takes it to be completely obvious that certain basic facts about the conditions of human existence must be added to the fundamental principle of morality to generate the duties of human beings (MMI, 6:216–17), but does not call this a "postulate." The "postulate of practical reason in regard to rights" (DR, §6, 6:250) to which Ripstein appeals is only that things other than human beings do not have any rights of their own that would preclude our use of them. I return to MMI, 6:216–17 in Section 3.1.

[18] Johnson (1996) argues that moral worth should be distinguished from the *merit* that Kant discusses at MMI, 6:227, which may attach to morally appropriate *actions* even without morally worthy motivation.

[19] For example, Wolfgang Kersting is confused by this into arguing that Kant does not derive Right from morals but from practical reason more generally, for example, Kersting (2004, p. 35). Mulholland is also not immune from confusing ethics with morality as a whole, for example, Mulholland (1990, p. 171). Even more than failing to recognize that Kant's special sense of *Moralität* is narrower than what we mean by morality as a whole, the real motivation for the independence thesis is the assumption that the categorical imperative requires that we act out of respect for the moral law, which Right does not. In Section I of the *Groundwork* (4:398), Kant uses examples of agents who act without any inclination and thus only from respect for the moral law to show that the law has nothing to do with inclination, and is instead purely formal, but once the law has been identified, it is always our duty to act in accordance with it, whether or not we earn the addition of moral worth by acting from the motivation of respect for the moral law. The latter is the special concern of Ethics in Kant's sense, but Right still requires that we act in conformity with the moral law, however we get ourselves to do it. Pauer-Studer (2016) is particularly clear on this point.

The Moral Foundation of Right

which anyone satisfies these obligations. This title itself implies that the juridical obligations of the domain of Right treated in the first half of the book are a proper part of what Kant calls "morals," even though they may be fulfilled without what *he* calls "morality" as the special and especially admirable condition of being motivated by the idea of duty itself.

Kant makes it clear that the duties of Right are part of morals in general with his further point that while only juridical duties or duties of Right can be incentivized with the external, aversive incentives – the threat of coercion – of a juridical system, *all* duties *can* be motivated by the ethical incentive of respect for the moral law. This is because all duties have their common source in the moral law, not in any other source. So Kant next writes that:

> Duties in accordance with rightful [*rechtlich*][20] lawgiving can be only external duties, since this lawgiving does not require that the idea of this duty, which is internal, itself be the determining ground of the agent's choice, and since it still needs an incentive suited to the law, it can connect only external incentives with the law. On the contrary, ethical lawgiving, while it also makes internal actions duties, does not exclude external actions but applies to everything that is a duty at all. (MMI, 6:219)

That is, since the threat of coercion can compel us to act in outward compliance with some requirements, for example, the prohibition of murder or fraud, but cannot make us act out of the "internal" motivation of respect for the moral law itself, juridical obligation, defined as it is by susceptibility to coercive enforcement, can concern only external actions, not the inner "action," that is, the motivation of respect for the moral law. But compliance with any and every moral obligation *could* be motivated by respect for the moral law, and in that sense compliance even with juridical obligations *can* be ethical, that is, motivated by respect for the moral law. Thus Kant says,

> It can be seen from this that all duties, just because they are duties, belong to ethics;[21] but it does not follow that the **lawgiving** for them is always

---

[20] "Rightful" may sound odd in English, but Kant's word *rechtlich* cannot be translated as "juridical," because he also uses the word *juridisch*, which obviously needs to be translated that way. "Righteous" could not be used either, because that suggests excessive pride in one's correct action, as in "self-righteous," which is certainly not any part of Kant's meaning.

[21] "*Ethik*," but in this case meaning "morals" in general, so translated here without the capital "E" that I will use in the rest of this passage. The "doctrine of virtue" to which Kant refers in a few lines refers to Ethics proper, that is, the noncoercively enforceable part of morals. It actually concerns two different kinds of duties, on the one hand all of our specific duties (*Tugendpflichten*) falling under the headings of the two "ends that are also duties" of self-perfection and promotion of the happiness of others (DV, Introduction, sections III-V, VIII), and the "obligation of virtue" (*Tugendverpflichtung*) to be motivated by respect for the moral law (see Guyer 2010). Kant might suggest that the specifically Ethical duties to adopt the ends of self-perfection and promoting the happiness of others can be motivated only by respect for the moral law, while the fulfillment of

contained in Ethics: for many of them it is outside of Ethics. Thus Ethics demands that I still fulfill a contract I have entered into ... but it takes the law (*pacta sunt servanda* [contracts are to be kept]) and the duty corresponding to it from the doctrine of Right, as already given there. Accordingly the giving of the law that promises agreed to must be kept lies not in Ethics but in *Ius* [that is, Right]. All that Ethics teaches is that if the incentive which juridical lawgiving connects with that duty, namely external constraint, were absent, the idea of duty by itself would be sufficient as an incentive. ... The doctrine of Right and the doctrine of virtue are therefore distinguished not so much by their different duties as by the difference in their lawgiving, which connects one incentive or the other with the law.

Ethical lawgiving (even if the duties might be external) is that which **cannot** be external; juridical lawgiving is that which can also be external. (MMI, 6:219–20).

There is room for confusion here, but the basic idea is clear. There is only one source of obligation, namely, the moral law. "Lawgiving," however, has two components, namely, the specific duties or types of duties that can be derived from the moral law, and the incentives that can motivate satisfaction of such duties.[22] Regarding the first component, there can be an exclusive distinction between duties of Ethics and duties of Right: juridical duties are those to which the external sanction of the threat of coercion can be attached, while ethical duties are those for which that is not the case. But as regards the second component, while only some duties, namely, those concerning external or outward conduct or actions, can possibly be motivated by external incentives or sanctions, all duties *can* be satisfied out of the motivation of sheer respect for the moral law. *This is possible only if even juridical duties have their source in the moral law* – otherwise how could respect for the moral law be a motive for fulfilling them? This, added to Kant's opening claim that all obligation arises from the one and only categorical imperative, clearly implies that for Kant duties of Right are part of what he calls morals in general, or what *we* call "morality," even though they can be fulfilled without that specific motivation that *he* calls "morality."

But all of this, as I said, remains at the level of formal or nominal definition. The actual content or substance of Kant's conception of duties of Right will

---

the duties of Right could be motivated by that or just by fear of threatened sanctions for noncompliance. The former is debatable, since one could at least act in outward compliance with the demands of self-perfection or the happiness of others out of self-love, for example, a concern for one's reputation; but what is important here is the latter, that it is morally appropriate and even necessary to enforce the demands of Right by coercive sanctions; see Guyer (2016b).

[22] This was clearly recognized in Gregor (1963, p. 26); Gregor calls the duties derived from the categorical imperative the material element of lawgiving, and the incentive of respect for the moral law required by Ethics only the formal element of ethical lawgiving.

provide a conclusive case for why they must be considered part of what Kant calls morals and we call morality in general, and why they cannot reasonably be regarded as having any other source.

3 Freedom, Morality, and Right: Kant's Core Argument

3.1 Kant's Substantive Definition of Right

Kant's substantive as opposed to formal definition of Right is "the sum of the conditions under which the choice of one can be united with the choice of the other [*des andern*][23] in accordance with a universal law of freedom." The "Universal Principle of Right" (*allgemeines Princip des Rechts*)[24] that he then formulates is that "Every action is **right** if [in] it or in accordance with its maxim the freedom of the power of choice of each can coexist [*zusammen bestehen*] with the freedom of everyone in accordance with a universal law" (DR, Introduction, sections B and C, 6:230). Kant makes similar statements in other sources. Thus, in his notes he defines Right by saying that "The doctrine of Right (as Right of human beings) is the content of laws without which freedom cannot subsist externally together with the freedom of everyone" (R 7309, 1780, 19:308; Kant 2016, p. 20), and in the transcription of his lectures on natural right he says that "Right is a limitation of freedom according to which freedom can coexist [*bestehen*] with the freedom of all others in accordance with a universal law" (L-NR, 27:1320; Kant 2016, p. 82). Right is thus the condition in which everyone can act as freely as possible consistently with the equal freedom of everyone else, and the principle of right – the categorical imperative of Right, if you will[25] – is to act only in ways – or only on maxims – that are consistent with the same, maximal degree of freedom for everyone else. Since in Kant's view the role of the state (*civitas*), which is itself defined as "a union of a multitude of human beings under laws of Right" (DR, §45, 6:313), is to make the condition of Right determinate and secure for the inhabitants of some bounded region of the surface of the earth, in light of these definitions the role of the state is nothing

---

[23] Both Gregor and Ladd translate *des andern* as "of another." In view of Kant's following statement of the "Universal Principle of Right," one might expect Kant to have written "of others" (*der anderen*) or "of all others" (*aller anderen*) here. I am suggesting "the other" here because that might be read generically, thus as "others" but not as "one other."

[24] The word *allgemein* could be translated as "general" as well as "universal," and it might be well to call Kant's principle the "general principle of Right" in order to suggest that more particular principles of Right, or of rights, will follow from it. But since in the preceding and succeeding statements the word *allgemein* has to be translated as "universal" in order for it to suggest, as Kant obviously intends, that the principle concerns the freedom of *everyone*, it seems better to follow Gregor and Ladd in translating it as "universal" in this occurrence also.

[25] This phrase is not Kant's, but is suggested by Höffe (1990, p. 126); in Höffe (2002, p. 85), it is translated as "categorical principle of law"

less and also nothing more than to make the conditions for the coexistence of the freedom of all, or as much freedom for each as is consistent with equal freedom for all, determinate and secure.[26] Thus Kant notes that "The state can coerce no one to be happy or to make another happy but must secure everyone's freedom" (R 7919, 1788–89, 19:554; Kant 2016, p. 48) and "Not the principle of general happiness but freedom according to universal laws constitutes the principle of the establishment of the state and its idea" (R 7955, 1780–84, 19:564; Kant 2016, p. 50).[27]

Drawing these thoughts together, Kant's first published exposition of his political philosophy in 1793 begins with this clear statement:

> But the concept of an external right as such proceeds entirely from the concept of **freedom** in the external relation of people to one another and has nothing at all to do with the end that all of them naturally have (their aim of happiness) and with the prescribing of means for attaining it; hence too the latter absolutely must not intrude in the laws of the former as their determining ground. **Right** is the limitation of the freedom of each to the condition of its harmony with the freedom of everyone insofar as this is possible in accordance with a universal law; and **public** Right is the sum of **external laws** which make such a thoroughgoing harmony possible. (TP, 8:289–90)

By "public Right" as the sum of "external laws" Kant means the state with its legislation defining the obligations and rights of its members, both citizens and office-holders. Thus Kant here clearly expresses his view that the function of the state is to establish and enforce, through its "positive" laws (DR, Introduction, section A, 6:229), that is, its actual legislation, the greatest freedom for each compatible with equal freedom for all in their interactions – that is the sense in which its laws are "external." But the positive law of any particular state, regardless of how it is actually made, needs to be justifiable in light of the Universal Principle of Right, and limited by it. Since the Universal Principle of Right is itself part of morality as a whole, this is how morality should apply to and govern the legislation of any actual state.

These definitions of Right and its Universal Principle demonstrate the foundation of the principle of Right in the fundamental principle of morality because the latter is itself nothing other than the demand for the preservation and promotion of maximal freedom of choice in one's own, intrapersonal case and maximal consistency of one's own exercise of freedom with the freedom of choice of all others in the interpersonal case. The principle of Right is just the

---

[26] That these are the primary functions of the state is frequently stressed in Ripstein (2009, beginning at p. 23).

[27] Again, this contrast has been widely recognized, for example, Gregor (1963, p. 26); Mulholland (1990, pp. 3–5); Ripstein (2009, pp. 2–3).

The Moral Foundation of Right

application of the fundamental principle of morality to the case in which one person's external use of choice – that is, action – has the potential to interfere with the free exercise of choice in the actions of others: in such cases the principle requires that each limit her exercise of choice – her freedom – to the condition of consistency with the exercise of free choice in action by all – but only by that condition. Only its threat to the freedom of others gives others the right to limit the freedom of action of anyone else.

Kant's insistence that the goal of the state is *not* the happiness of its members but their freedom – which they can use within its limits of equality with the freedom of others to realize their own happiness as they choose, or not at all – provides further evidence that its foundation can lie only in morality itself. For in the *Groundwork for the Metaphysics of Morals* Kant insists that there are really only two kinds of principles of practical reason, that is, the application of reason to action, on the one hand "counsels" of prudence, "of diet, frugality, courtesy, reserve, and so forth, which experience teaches us are most conducive to well-being on the average" (G, 4:418), that is, which are the deliverances of the empirical use of practical reason, or, on the other hand, the sole imperative of pure practical reason, the fundamental principle of morality. Since the fundamental principle of politics is not prudence, it can be grounded only in the fundamental principle of morality itself. For Kant there is no middle ground between prudence and morality or any third form of practical reason.[28] Or perhaps better, for Kant the ground for accepting the rule of the state cannot be *mere* prudence, for even though in many situations prudence and morality may call for the same course of action, they are not the same and will not always call for the same course of action. The demands of morality sometimes override mere prudence, or prudent self-love, so morality cannot be founded on mere prudence, and therefore neither can Right.[29]

Although Kant's fundamental dichotomy between prudence and morality is clear in the *Groundwork*, that the fundamental principle of morality itself is nothing other than the command for maximal consistency in the intra- and interpersonal use of freedom may not be so clear in that work, in Kant's other foundational work in moral philosophy, namely, the *Critique of Practical*

---

[28] This is why Kersting's strategy of deriving Right from pure practical reason but not from morality is misleading; for Kant pure practical reason and morality are equivalent, and the only other form of practical reason is empirical, that is, mere counsels of prudence. See Kersting (2004, pp. 21–31).

[29] That prudence *often* suggests accepting the rule of the state is the germ of truth in Hobbes's argument, but for him prudence is the supreme principle, thus one *always* retains the right of self-defense against the state (*Leviathan*, chapter 14; in Hobbes 2012, vol. 2, p. 214). For Kant, prudent self-love does not reign supreme, and sometimes preserving maximal possible freedom for all might require self-sacrifice (e.g., DV, §6, 6:423).

Reason, or even in the Introduction to the *Metaphysics of Morals*. So the first step in my argument must be to show that the requirement for the greatest possible consistency in the intra- and interpersonal use of freedom is indeed Kant's fundamental principle of morality, so that the Universal Principle of Right's demand for the great possible consistency in the external, interpersonal use of freedom is indeed just an implication or simply a part of that general principle.

We can work back from the Introduction to the *Metaphysics of Morals*. Kant first argues that moral laws "hold as laws only insofar as they can be **seen** to have an *a priori* basis and to be necessary" and "command for everyone, without taking account of inclinations, merely because and insofar as [they are] free and [have] practical reason" (MMI, 6:215–16), and then states that "a metaphysics of morals cannot dispense with principles of application," for which we shall "have to take as our object the particular **nature** of human beings, which is cognized only by experience, in order to **show** in it what can be inferred from universal moral principles" (6:217). This means that the fundamental principle of morality must be entirely a priori, derived from pure reason alone, but that certain basic but only empirically known and therefore contingent facts about human nature and the human condition are necessary for the derivation of the specific duties of human beings, including the duties of Right from the a priori principle of morality in general that is valid for all rational beings.[30] Kant then proceeds to a systematic exposition of "The Preliminary Concepts of the Metaphysics of Morals." This begins with the statements that "The concept of **freedom** is a pure rational concept," the concept of the "causality of pure reason for determining choice independently of any empirical conditions," and that "On this concept of freedom, which is positive (from a practical point of view), are based unconditional practical laws, which are called **moral**" (MMI, 6:221). All of this might mean only, as it did for other authors of the period, that the subject matter of morality is the actions of free agents, or the free actions of agents – not the motions or behavior of nonfree agents, such as falling stones or what we take other animals to be, nor the involuntary actions of persons, as when they are pushed by someone else – but not to imply that the preservation and promotion of freedom is the *goal* of morality.[31] And when Kant introduces the concept of a categorical imperative

---

[30] Thus other sorts of rational beings, if there are any, would still be subject to the same general principle of morality but might have different sorts of duties than humans do.

[31] For example, Pufendorf (2003, Book I, chapter I, paragraph II); Thomasius (2011, §55); Baumgarten (2020, §11); Achenwall (2020a, §7). Among these, perhaps Baumgarten's statement prepares the way for Kant's conception of the goal of morality: "There can be no obligation where there is no freedom; therefore obligation cannot destroy freedom, nor is it its opposite, but is rather its consequence and implication" (Baumgarten 2020, p. 40).

into his exposition, which is defined as a "morally practical **law**" that "asserts an obligation with respect to certain actions" but also connotes the existence of "**necessitation**" or constraint because it "either commands or prohibits" such actions to creatures, like us, who do not always naturally incline to fulfill their obligations but at least sometimes resist them (MMI, 6:222–3; cf. G, 4:412), his first formulation of the categorical imperative, as in the *Groundwork* and *Critique of Practical Reason*, invokes only the necessary universal validity of our maxims of action, as what pure practical reason must demand: "The categorical imperative, which as such only affirms what obligation is, is: act upon a maxim that can also hold as a universal law."

> You must therefore first consider your actions in terms of their subjective principles; but you can know whether this principle also holds objectively only in this way: that when your reason subjects it to the test of conceiving yourself as also giving universal law through it, it qualifies for such a giving of universal law. (6:225)

That is, it is morally permissible to act on some maxim only if it would continue to be possible to act on that maxim if it were universalized, or if everyone were to act on it. (This is what is known as the "Formula of Universal Law.") In Kant's best known and most workable example: if you propose to get money by making a false promise, one that you do not intend to keep, could you still accomplish your purpose if everyone were to adopt such a maxim? No, because under that condition, no one would accept a promise, the institution of promising would collapse, and your proposed action would become impossible. Therefore your action would be morally impermissible: you could not will both your proposed maxim and its universalization.[32] However, even though this formulation of the categorical imperative applies only to beings capable of free choice, it makes no direct reference to freedom at all, that is, it does not explicitly prescribe the preservation and promotion of free choice or action upon free choice. The same is true of Kant's next statement, that "The supreme principle of the doctrine of morals, is therefore, act on a maxim which can also hold as a universal law. – Any action that does not so qualify is contrary to morals" (6:226).

But Kant's formulations of the definition of Right and the Universal Principle of Right *do* explicitly refer to freedom, namely, to the necessity of the coexistence

---

[32] See O'Neill (2013, chapter 5); Rawls (1989, pp. 498–501), where Rawls introduces the term "CI-Procedure," and Rawls (2000, pp. 167–72); Korsgaard (1996, pp. 92–4). The question here is not the empirical question whether your acting on some maxim would in fact lead all others to act upon it, and whether you would like that, but the hypothetical question whether your proposed action would even be possible *if* everyone were to act upon it, and whether you *could* continue to will to act upon it subject to that condition. Prudence does not require that you ask the hypothetical question, since sometimes you might know that you could act in a certain way without others also doing so; it is morality that requires you to ask that question.

of any one person's exercise of freedom with the exercise of freedom by all. So how can his principle of Right be derived from the fundamental principle of morality, or from its presentation to us sometimes recalcitrant human beings in the form of the categorical imperative? The answer to this question lies in Kant's statement that "The ground of the possibility of categorical imperatives is this: that they relate to no other property of choice (by which some intention [*Absicht*] can be imputed to it) than merely to its **freedom**" (MMI, 6:222). That is, the categorical imperative – or, since Kant uses the plural, any specific versions of the categorical imperative – does not simply *presuppose* the freedom of the agents to which it applies; it concerns *only* their freedom – what it prescribes is nothing less and nothing more than the universalization *of their freedom*. The categorical imperative requires that anyone exercise their freedom – expressed in their choice of maxims for their actions – only in ways consistent with the freedom of everyone else. And this is exactly what the Universal Principle of Right requires in the case of any and all of our actions that could interfere with the freedom of choice of action by others.

3.2 Earlier Versions of Kant's Argument

This might seem like a lot to extract from Kant's remark that the "ground of the possibility of categorical imperatives" "relates" "merely" to freedom. But if we now go back to look at Kant's statements about the fundamental principle of morality and the categorical imperative in works leading up to the *Metaphysics of Morals* we will see that this is what he means. Kant uses a variety of concepts to express the fundamental principle of morality, but they all point in the same direction. Whether Kant presents the principle in terms of will, willing maxims, humanity, or freedom of choice, the result is always that the fundamental principle of morality is to preserve and promote the greatest and most equal freedom of choice of ends and action toward those ends that is possible for oneself and others. The principle of Right is simply that such freedom must be preserved in the subset of cases in which one person's choices of action would leave others with less freedom than the first would enjoy, so the principle of Right is simply part of the principle of morality itself.[33]

---

[33] Kant himself assumes that the possibility of morality depends upon a libertarian conception of freedom of the will, that is, an absolute freedom to choose either of two alternatives regardless of everything about one's prior history, a possibility that he argues in the first two critiques can be defended only by means of his distinction between how things appear, namely, as entirely causally determined, and how they may be in themselves, namely spontaneous. This is the view that he calls "transcendental idealism," and it remains deeply controversial. (For my criticism of transcendental idealism, see Guyer 1987 and 2017; for defense, see Allison 2004.) But the normative contents of his theory of Right and of morality as a whole do not depend upon this conception of free will. The doctrine of Right requires only the conception of freedom as the

Kant's earliest recorded thoughts about morality are notes that he made in his own copy of his 1764 book *Observations on the Feeling of the Beautiful and Sublime*.[34] One of these notes says that "In subjection there is not only something externally dangerous but also a certain ugliness and contradiction that at the same time indicates its unlawfulness.... [T]hat the human being himself should have no will of its own, and that another soul should move my limbs, is absurd and perverse" (ROFBS, 20:93; Kant 2011, p. 129). Kant's observation that there is "something externally dangerous" in subjection may be taken to acknowledge that it is in fact often imprudent or risky to try to subject others to one's own will rather than finding a way to minimize subjection to all. In surrounding remarks Kant also suggests that there is something psychologically displeasing about the subjection of one human being to the will of another: we may chafe at the limitations nature places on us,

> But what is much harder and more unnatural than this yoke of necessity is the subjection of one human being under the will of another human being. There is no misfortune more terrible to him who would be accustomed to freedom. ... If I was free before, nothing can present a more dreadful prospect of sorrow and despair than that in the future my state shall not reside in my own will, but in the will of another. (20:92; pp. 127–8)

But Kant's use of terms of *logical* criticism – "contradiction" and "absurd" – as he continues suggests that there is more than an argument from prudence or psychology here. Rather, Kant suggests that all humans being *do* have wills of their own; that we all *know* this; that to subject others to one's own will is to *treat* them as if they did *not* have wills of their own, which is in turn tantamount to *denying* that they have their own wills; thus in subjecting others to our own will we are both asserting and denying that they have wills of their own – which is a contradiction, a violation of the most fundamental law of reason. In various forms, an argument like this remains the most basic level of Kant's thought about morality.[35]

---

ability to set and pursue one's own ends without domination by other persons (see also Ripstein 2009, p. 42), and morality as a whole requires only the further conception of freedom as independence from domination by one's own inclinations. Whether human beings are always free to make the morally correct choice and can be held responsible for their actions only if that is so are separate questions that I will not further discuss in this Element. Thus I disagree with the interpretation that Kant's conception of Right presupposes his transcendental idealist conception of freedom of the will, for example, Kersting (2004, p. 24). For my general treatment of Kant on freedom of the will, see Guyer (2014, chapter 6, pp. 245–65), and Guyer (2016a, chapters 8–11); for an outstanding work on the subject, see Timmermann (2022).

[34] They are translated in part in Kant (2005, pp. 1–24), in their entirety in Kant (2011, pp. 65–202).
[35] See Guyer (2019, pp. 12–34).

The next major source for Kant's evolving moral philosophy is the lectures on ethics that are recorded from the middle of the 1770s.[36] In the introductory section on "The Supreme Principle of Morality," Kant states that this principle must be "intellectual" – what he will subsequently call a priori rather than *a posteriori* or empirical – and offers what is clearly a version of his later first formulation of the categorical imperative: "The principle of morality is the agreement of an action with a universally valid law of the free power of choice" (Eth-K, pp. 64–5). Kant continues:

> In all moral judgments we frame the thought: how would the action be if it were taken universally? If the intention of the action would agree with itself if it were made into a universal rule, then the action is morally possible; if the intention of the action would not agree with itself if it were made universal, then the action is morally impossible.... That is therefore an immoral action the intention of which would suspend and destroy itself if it were made into a universal rule. (Eth-K, p. 67)

Here, as O'Neill, Rawls, and Korsgaard have suggested, the contradiction is between an intention and its supporting maxim and the universalization of that maxim, as in Kant's example of the contradiction between the intention to accomplish some end by making a false promise and the consequences of the universalization of the supporting maxim of lying in order to achieve one's ends. But why should one raise a moral question about the consequences of the universalization of one's own maxim in the actual world, in which the universalization of one's maxim might not result from one's own adoption of it? Kant's introductory discussion might suggest that pure reason simply requires universalizability, and many commentators on Kant have been content with that idea.[37] But in the main part of the lectures, Kant suggests that the core concept of morality is "freedom according to a choice that is not necessitated," that is freedom of choice, because freedom is "the highest degree of life ... the inner worth of the world, the *summum bonum*." Yet precisely in order to maximize

---

[36] One version of these lectures is a transcription from the summer semester of 1777 that bears the name of Johann Friedrich Kaehler, first published in 2004 (Eth-K). A previously published transcription bearing the name of Georg Ludwig Collins and the date "Winter Semester 1784–85" is largely identical to the notes by Kaehler but differs significantly from another set by Carl Coelestin Mrongrovious that is also labeled "Winter Semester" with the particular date January 3, 1785 (these notes are known as "Mrongovius II," found at Kant 1900–, vol. 29, pp. 597–642; pp. 597–633 translated in Kant 1997). Mrongovius's introduction uses the language of Kant's *Groundwork*, published that spring, so his notes presumably represent what Kant was actually saying that winter while Collins must have copied his notes from an earlier source corresponding to Kaehler's source. Both the Kaehler and Collins notes can therefore be used to interpret the development of Kant's thought in the 1770s, the "silent decade" during which he was working on the *Critique of Pure Reason* but published almost nothing (see Werkmeister 1979; Guyer 1987, Part I; and Carl 1989).

[37] For example, Wood (2008, pp. 16–17); Korsgaard (2009, p. 73).

that value, to prevent any one exercise of freedom of choice from undermining and destroying the possibility of others, which would be "the most terrible thing there could ever be," or "savage disorder," freedom must be "restricted by objective rules" (Eth-K, p. 177; *Collins*, 27:344). These "objective rules," however, although Kant refers to them in the plural, are in fact nothing but the single principle that every use of freedom, every free choice, must be compatible with the greatest possible use of freedom. In this section, Kant is discussing duties to oneself, and the rule for "self-regarding actions" is "so to behave that any use of [one's] powers is compatible with the greatest possible use of them because "the greatest use of freedom" is "the highest *principium* of life. Only under certain conditions can freedom be consistent with itself; otherwise it comes into contradiction with itself." For example, the decision to get drunk might be a free choice considered by itself, but it can destroy one's ability to make further free choices for a time, or, if one maims or kills oneself in an ensuing car crash, one's free choice can limit or completely destroy one's further possibility of freedom. But this example immediately suggests that this principle is not in fact just self-regarding, for obviously a drunk driver can injure or kill others and thereby limit or altogether destroy *their* freedom. Thus the restriction of any use of one's freedom to the "conditions under which alone the greatest use of freedom is possible, and under which it can be self-consistent," is entirely general and the "*principium* of all duties," not just duties to oneself (Eth-K, pp. 179–80; Eth-C, 27:346). It applies to the interpersonal and intrapersonal case, and is the fundamental principle of morality for both.[38] Further, although Kant is not discussing Right here, his example also shows clearly why the fundamental principle of governmental regulation, the principle of Right, is implicit in the fundamental principle of morality: we all assume that government should prohibit driving under the influence precisely because one individual's choice to drive while drunk, although considered by itself perhaps a free choice, can easily damage or completely destroy the freedom of others and is therefore not consistent with the "greatest use of freedom." If driving while drunk risked injury only to one's own freedom, perhaps we would not feel comfortable publicly enforcing its prohibition; but since it clearly risks injury to the freedom of others, we have no hesitation in doing so.

But now what has happened to the first formulation of the categorical imperative as the requirement to act only on maxims that could also be willed to be universal laws? To answer this question we need to understand the structure of

---

[38] In Mrongovius II, Kant says "The principle of freedom is the principle of external freedom, the restriction of freedom under the condition whereby alone it can co-exist with that of everyone else" (Kant 1900–, 29:632).

Kant's argument in Section II, the central section of the *Groundwork for the Metaphysics of Morals*. Here Kant first formulates the categorical imperative as the command to act only on universalizable maxims, but then argues that the *ground* of the categorical imperative is the "humanity" (*Menschheit*) in every person. However, this humanity includes the capacity of each person to set her own ends, which is the form of freedom relevant to Right.[39] Thus, although now under the name of humanity, the intrinsic and unconditional value of free choice, of all of one's own free choice but of everyone's else's free choice equally, remains the fundamental value underlying all formulations of the categorical imperative, and the rule of acting only on universalizable maxims becomes a means of realizing this end. When he comes to the *Doctrine of Right*, Kant then appeals directly to the obligation on every person to treat the humanity in every person always as an end and never merely a means as the foundation of Right, in this way showing that Right is founded in the foundational value of morality just as the categorical imperative formulated as the requirement that one's maxims be universalizable is.

Kant begins his argument in the *Groundwork* with an argument by elimination: if a categorical imperative as a necessarily true law that can be known by pure reason a priori can contain no contingent and therefore empirical "condition to which it would be limited," then "nothing is left with which the maxim of action is to conform but the universality of a law as such, and this conformity alone is what the imperative properly represents as necessary."[40]

---

[39] Nance (2012) also identifies humanity as the capacity to set our own ends as the moral basis of Right. Nance emphasizes that Right follows from the categorical imperative for embodied agents: a person's ability to do what she pleases with her body, within the confines of universal law, is part of the capacity for humanity itself. This is one way of understanding what Kant means by the phrase "freedom in the *external* use of choice" (p. 548).

[40] Pauer-Studer (2016) similarly says that the "Formula of Universal Law ... comes up at the end of a regressive argument intended to identify the principle underlying the good will" p. 143; this refers to the starting point of Kant's preliminary presentation in section I of the proper metaphysics of morals to be presented in section II of the *Groundwork*. Apart from Nance (2012), Pauer-Studer's paper comes closer than anything else in the recent literature to the view presented here; thus she writes that "autonomy of the person in the sense of self-determination by rational willing amounts to a basic presupposition of Kant's ethics" (in the general sense) and that "Our recognition of the value of humanity and autonomy provides us with a normative reason to consent to the principles that are constitutive of autonomy in the sphere[s] of inner and outer freedom," that is, in Ethics properly speaking and Right (p. 146). The difference between her approach and mine is that she sees Kant's idea of a "realm of ends" as the most basic expression of the underlying value, from which Kant then works back to the idea of humanity as an end in itself and from there to the Formula of Universal Law as the "testing procedure for maxims" (p. 150), whereas on my view the unconditional value of humanity, *whether in one's own person or that of any other*, already implies that the realm (or as I prefer to call it "empire" of ends" must be the *object* of morality and the universalizability of maxims the "testing procedure." On the "empire of ends," see Guyer (2022a).

There is, therefore, only a single categorical imperative, and it is this: **act only in accordance with that maxim through which you can at the same time will that it become a universal law**. (G, 4:421)

However, in the *Critique of Pure Reason* Kant insists that "transcendental proofs" – the proofs that go to the very conditions of the possibility of knowledge, whether theoretical or practical, thus including knowledge of the fundamental principle of morality – "must never be **apagogic** but always **ostensive**." By "apagogic" proofs he means indirect proofs such as proofs by elimination, while by "ostensive" proofs he means "direct" proofs that are "combined with the conviction or proof and simultaneously with insight into its sources" (CPR, A 789/B 817). In other words, philosophy ultimately requires proofs that show not just *that* something is true, on the assumption that the proof has accounted for all possibilities and eliminated all but one of them, but that also show *why* it is true. Apagogic proofs "can produce certainty, to be sure, but never comprehensibility of the truth in regard to the grounds of its possibility," yet philosophy requires such comprehensibility. For this reason, after formulating the categorical imperative as the Formula of Universal Law, Kant says that we must nevertheless, "however reluctantly, step forth, namely into ... metaphysics of morals" (G, 4:427) and find something that could be "the ground of a possible categorical imperative." This, he says, must be "something the **existence of which in itself** has an absolute worth, namely something which as an **end in itself** could be a ground of determinate laws" (4:428).

Now where have we previously heard about something the existence of which in itself has an "absolute worth"? Of course, in the statement in the lectures that freedom is the "inner worth of the world" – except what Kant now says is that "the human being and in general every rational being **exists** as an end in itself, **not merely as a means** to be by used by this or that will at its discretion" (G, 4:428), and what he infers from this is that "The practical imperative will therefore be the following: **So act that you use humanity, whether in your own person or in the person of any other, always as an end, never merely as a means**" (4:429; this is known as the "Formula of Humanity as an End in Itself"). But what Kant means by "humanity" here is precisely the capacity to set one's own ends, to freely choose the ends of one's actions, and the Formula of Humanity as an End in Itself therefore means that in any exercise of one's free choice preserving and promoting one's own capacity for such choice *and* that of every other person must be one's overriding end, whatever more particular goal one might have in mind. As Kant says in the *Groundwork*, "Rational nature is distinguished from the rest of nature by this, that it sets itself an end" (G, 4:437), so to make rational nature, or better rational *agency*, which we are acquainted with only in the case of humankind, thus in the form of humanity, our end is to make the *capacity to set ends* our most general end.[41] Or, as Kant says even more directly in the *Metaphysics of Morals*, humanity is that "by which" a human being "alone is capable of setting himself ends" (DV, Introduction, section V.A, 6:387), or "the capacity to set oneself an end – any end whatsoever – is what characterizes humanity (as distinct from animality)" (Section VIII, 6:392). The capacity to freely choose our own ends and the actions by which to realize them is the end in itself, the inner worth of the world – but this capacity not just on one occasion of use, but throughout one's life, and not just in oneself, but in everyone. To treat this capacity in this way of course requires "objective rules" of "consistency," and therefore the use of reason, but not merely instrumental reason, or counsels of prudence.[42]

In the *Groundwork*, Kant does not offer an argument for the claim that rational nature, or its sole known instantiation in the form of humanity, is the one and only end in itself. He simply says that the nature of human beings as "persons," beings that can set their own ends, "already marks them out as an end in itself, that is, as something that may not be used merely as a means, and hence so far limits all choice" (G, 4:429). Just as he earlier supposed that it is self-evident that every human being has her own will and that we cannot deny this without contradicting ourselves, so he now also supposes that it is self-evident that every human being has the capacity to set her own ends, leaving unstated that we cannot deny this without contradicting ourselves. Nor does Kant offer much explanation of how

---

[41] One of the best brief interpretations of Kant's moral philosophy in recent literature is Klemme (2023). The difference between his approach and mine is that on his account the goal of morality is the "self-preservation of reason" or rationality in general, whereas on mine it is the preservation (and promotion) of rational *agency*, the capacity to set our own ends, although to be sure in a rational way.

[42] There has been extensive debate whether the ultimate object of value is rationality itself (see Timmermann 2007, p. 96, and Klemme 2023), actually being moral (Dean 2006), our capacity for morality (Allison 2011), or simply our capacity to set our own ends – that "humanity is the capacity to exercise freedom in a being in the world" (Mulholland 1990, p. 209). Actually being moral would preclude some people much of the time and most people some of the time from being objects of moral regard, which is certainly not what Kant intends (see Wood 1999, pp. 134, 153, 407n32); and no doubt the capacity to be moral is part of the capacity to be rational, and what gives us our "dignity" (G, 4:435); but to treat humanity *only* as the capacity to be moral would risk circularity and provide no content, or insufficient content, to the command to make humanity our overriding end. It may well be that it is our capacity for morality that gives us dignity and makes us worthy of moral regard (see G, 4:435), but morality needs some content if the concept of the capacity for morality is not to be vacuous. The concept of humanity as the freedom to set our own ends gives the command to make it our end and never merely a means content and thereby gives content to the concept of morality itself. In *Religion within the Boundaries of Mere Reason*, Kant distinguishes humanity from "personality," and clearly identifies only the latter with the capacity to be moral (Rel, 6:26–7). If we want, we could interpret humanity in the *Groundwork* as including both humanity and personality as defined in the *Religion*, but it has at least to include the capacity to set our own ends to give morality any content.

precisely the status of humanity as an end in itself, and the only one, "grounds the possibility" of the previous formulation of the categorical imperative as the requirement to act only on maxims that we could also will to be universal laws. Presumably he supposes that if everyone could choose to act on a maxim on which we choose to act, that means that our choice leaves them as free to choose that maxim as we are. This would leave them free not to do what we are doing, after all, but if they were to consider acting in circumstances like our own of course they would also have to act only on a universalizable maxim. This would be the sense in which the Formula of Universal Law could be a "testing procedure" for the Formula of Humanity as an End in Itself. But this step need not detain us, because the key point here is that *Kant derives the Universal Principle of Right directly from the status of humanity as an end in itself,* not from the Formula of Universal Law. The fact of our common humanity, in Kant's special sense, is the foundation of the Universal Principle of Right, just as this fact is the ground of the categorical imperative in general.

The *Feyerabend* lectures, delivered at the very time that Kant was writing the *Groundwork*, suggest the same conclusion. Initially ignoring his textbook, Kant began with an exposition of the main ideas of his own moral philosophy as it was taking shape in the *Groundwork*. Kant's introduction takes up ten printed pages (L-NR, 27:1319–29), and seems to have stretched over several sessions. That Kant began with this general exposition of his own moral philosophy itself, just as he would later do in the *Metaphysics of Morals*, makes clear that he regarded his topic as a proper part of moral philosophy. The lectures begin with the assertion that "The whole of nature is subject to the will of a human being as far as his power can reach excepting other human beings and rational beings. Considered rationally, things in nature can be viewed only as means to ends but a human being alone can be viewed as himself an end" (27:1319). Kant then hints at his original idea that since we know this perfectly well it is a contradiction for us to act in a way that effectively denies it: "A human being is an end so it is contradictory to say that a human being should be a mere means" (27:1319). This is the bedrock of Kant's moral thought. Kant then spells out that the status of all human beings as ends in themselves is based on the possession by each of his or her own will, but he identifies having a will of one's own with freedom, thus tying together the terminology of his original notes, of his lectures on ethics from the previous decade, and of the *Groundwork*: will is freedom which is the end in itself. As he does in the *Groundwork* (G, 4:434–5), Kant also links our having our own wills with our unique "dignity," unlike everything else in nature that has merely a "price":

> To be precise a human being is an end in itself, from this a human being can have only an inner value, i.e., have a dignity in whose place no equivalent can

> be set. Other things have outer value, i.e., price, for which each and every thing that is fitting for the same end can be set as an equivalent. <u>The inner value of a human being is based on his freedom, that he has a will of his own.</u> Because he should be the final end his will must be dependent on nothing else. – An animal has a will but it does not have a will of its own but the will of nature. The freedom of a human being is the condition under which a human being can himself be an end. (27:1319–20)

Freedom is nonfungible: freedom, unlike anything else, cannot be traded off for something else of equal value. There is nothing else of equal value. But if each human being possesses freedom and is therefore entitled to the status of an end in itself, then the value of freedom will be fully realized only if the freedom of each human being is exercised only in ways that are compatible with the freedom of all. And then Kant concludes that "Right is a limitation of freedom according to which freedom can coexist with the freedom of all others in accordance with a universal law" (27:1320): the definition of Right that he uses in his final statement of the doctrine of Right is reached at the end of this argument.

Kant concluded his first lecture in *Feyerabend* by distinguishing his approach to morality in general and to Right in particular from the standard approach, which grounded morality and Right in the supposed value of happiness:

> Freedom must thus be limited but this cannot be done through natural laws, for otherwise the human being would not be free, thus he must limit himself. Right thus depends upon the limitation of freedom. . . . – Happiness does not come into consideration at all with regard to right for each can try to attain happiness however he wants (27:1321) –

as long, that is, as one person's way of pursing happiness does not prejudice the *freedom* of others. Behind this passage there are at least three thoughts. First, the law that limits our use of freedom to its use consistent with the freedom of all is a law of reason, not mere nature – although in light of Kant's claim in the *Groundwork* that our nature "marks us out" as ends in ourselves, reason must be part of *our* nature. Second, our freedom to set our own ends is the condition of the *possibility* of our pursuit of happiness, because happiness is nothing other than the realization of our ends (G, 4:418). But, third, precisely because we can each use our freedom to set *different* ends than others, as long as they do not compromise the freedom of others, there can be no single conception of happiness that is universally valid, and therefore the pursuit of happiness cannot be the fundamental principle and direct object of morality, a fortiori of Right. Morality in general and Right in particular do not *preclude* the pursuit of happiness by anyone, because since happiness is the realization of our ends, our freedom as the freedom to set our own ends *is* freedom to pursue our own conception of happiness; but any one person's exercise of her freedom to set and pursue her own ends must always be constrained by the equal value of the freedom of everyone to do the same.

Kant reiterates his basic idea in what appears to have been the next lecture, summing up his argument thus far with the remark that "If rational beings alone are capable of being ends in themselves it cannot be because they have reason but because they have freedom. Reason is merely a means" (27:1321). That is, reason is what we need to use in order to exercise our own freedom and set our own ends only in ways that are compatible with the equal freedom of all to do the same. This tells us in a nutshell that a pure principle of rationality such as the Formula of Universal Law is in fact but the means to realize the value of freedom. This is why Kant at this point invokes the contemporaneous *Groundwork*'s distinction between two kinds of "hypothetical" imperatives, those of "skill" and of "prudence" (although at G, 4:418 he denies that the latter are really imperatives at all) on the one hand, and the one and only categorical imperative on the other (27:1323–4): the use of the latter is the means to freedom as the end, just as the other forms of imperatives – which of course are not really imperatives after all – express the means to other, lesser, contingent ends. Kant then introduces his students to the formal distinction between Right and Ethics just as it will subsequently be made in the *Metaphysics of Morals*. Obligation in general rests on "the possibility for how the action can hold under universal laws." "Legality is agreement of an action with duty" or obligation "without considering whether or not duty is the determining ground of the action," that is, the agent's fundamental motivation, thus an action is legal just as long as it conforms with obligation. And "Morality is the agreement of an action with duty insofar as duty is the determining ground of the action," that is, insofar as respect or esteem for duty is itself the motivation for fulfilling one's obligation. Kant then distinguishes Right from Ethics on the basis of this distinction: "In all juridical actions their legality is conformity with duty, but not their morality, they are not done from duty. Legality is only concerned with whether I act in conformity with duty, beyond that it is all the same whether I act out of respect or inclination or fear." Kant makes it clear that this is the basis of the distinction between Right and Ethics properly so called: "Ethics (*Ethic*) is the science of judging an action in accordance with its morality. *Jus* [Right] is the science of judging an action in accordance with its legality. Ethics is also called the doctrine of virtue" (all from 27:1327). The crucial point here, again, is that the distinction between legality and morality, between Right and Ethics, is a distinction *within* morals as a whole. There has been no suggestion that Right has any other foundation than the general premise that human freedom is the end in it itself that Kant has been expounding up to this point. It is crucial to keep this in mind when reading the *Doctrine of Right* published a dozen years later. There Kant does not repeat the introductory argument of the lectures, but must have felt that he had no need to because in the interim he had published the *Groundwork for the Metaphysics of Morals*. Everyone could now read the foundations that he still had to lay out for his students in the summer of 1784.

Finally, as he does in the *Metaphysics of Morals*, Kant informs his students that *Jus* or Right concerns those actions that can be coerced, while "Ethics is not concerned with actions that can be coerced." He explains that "Ethics is the practical philosophy of action regarding dispositions," that is, fundamental motivation, while "*Jus* is the practical philosophy of actions regardless of dispositions." "Everything obligatory belongs to Ethics, thus all duties," because *any* obligation *can* be fulfilled entirely on the basis of respect for the moral law itself, but "*Jus* is concerned with duties and actions that are in accord with the law and can be coerced. . . . Right is a doctrine of duties that can and should be coerced through force" (27:1327). Kant then asks his students, "When is an action enforceable?" (27:1328). Well, if it is duty but "respect for the law" is not a sufficient motive for someone to do it, "then it must be done through coercion" (27:1327). But if "Coercion is a limitation of freedom," how can the use of coercion ever be right? Because, as Kant has already argued, the use of freedom must be compatible with the greatest possible freedom for everyone: it is only the use of freedom in accordance with a universal law, not freedom without any constraint at all, that is permitted and required by the fundamental principle of morality. "An action that is directed in accordance with a universal rule of freedom is right, [but] if it contradicts freedom in accordance with a universal rule then it is unjust. The aim may be whatever it will. My action is allowed to be constituted only in a way that accords with universal freedom" (27:1328). Again, Kant appeals to logic, that is, to pure reason: if an action contradicts the universal rule of freedom, it is wrong, but upholding the universal rule of freedom, that is, preserving the greatest freedom equally possible for all, even if it involves the use of coercion, is right.

3.3 Kant's Final Version of His Argument in the *Doctrine of Right*

In the *Feyerabend* lectures, Kant's proof that Right is as much a part of morals as is Ethics is based on the premise that freedom is the end, reason the means. In the *Doctrine of Right*, Kant adopts the style of the *Groundwork* by basing his argument for the Universal Principle of Right on the foundational value that grounds morals in general, the status of humanity as an end in itself: since humanity is or includes the freedom of each human to set her own ends, its status as end in itself requires the adoption of the principle that everyone should have as much freedom as is possible consistent with the equal freedom of everyone else. The structure of Kant's argument in the Introduction to the *Doctrine of Right* closely follows the structure of his argument in the central

The Moral Foundation of Right

section of the *Groundwork*, and ultimately rests on the same premise as the latter: the intrinsic and unconditional value of humanity as an end in itself.

As we have already seen, Kant defines the doctrine of Right as the "sum of those laws for which an external lawgiving is possible," and states that the "doctrine of natural Right" "must supply the immutable principles for any giving of positive law" (DR, Introduction, Section A, 6:229). A doctrine of natural Right is to supply the moral standard by which the actual legislation – positive law – of any particular regime is to be evaluated and if necessary reformed. The possibility of external lawgiving is a formal and nominal definition of Right. Kant next provides his substantive definition of Right: "Right is ... the sum of the conditions under which the choice of one can be united with the choice of another in accordance with a universal law of freedom" (Section B, 6:230), that is, not just a law for free beings, but the law that freedom itself must be universal. Kant then applies this definition to the case of particular actions in the form of the Universal Principle of Right, "Any action is **right** if it can coexist with everyone's freedom or if on its maxim the freedom of the choice of each can coexist with everyone's freedom in accordance with a universal law" (Section C, 6:230). This still has the form of a definition.[43]

So does Kant's next step, the introduction of the concept of *strict* Right. Kant defines "strict Right" as "the possibility of thoroughly reciprocal coercion compatible with everyone's freedom in accordance with universal laws" (Section E, 6:232).[44] This is an analytic proposition because it has been reached from the previous definition of right as the use of freedom in accordance with universal law by what Kant regards as a strictly logical step, namely, the connection of "authorization to coerce someone who infringes upon" Right "by the principle of contradiction." His argument is that since the use of freedom in accordance with universal law is right, then whatever is "a hindrance to freedom in accordance with universal laws" is wrong, but then whatever is a hindrance to *that*, thus a **"hindering of a hindrance to freedom,"** is once again right (Section D, 6:231). Actually, what Kant is using is the principle of double negation, that a double negation is an affirmation ($\neg(\neg p) = p$), but this is still a purely logical principle, and Kant's connection of the right to use coercion to prevent violation of Right is still supposed to follow from the definition of

---

[43] Although the assumption that there can be such a condition of coexistence is the "postulate" that inclines Ripstein to call the Universal Principle of Right an "extension" rather than mere "application" of the categorical imperative (Ripstein 2009, pp. 361, 264–5).

[44] Gregor translates Kant's definition using "a strict right" as a variable for any particular enforceable right, although Kant's own text continues the collective form of his initial definitions. Ladd translates "strict right" as "justice (in the strict sense), but also uses "justice [or a right]." But for Kant, "strict Right" denotes the totality of our coercibly enforceable rights.

Right plus a purely logical principle.[45] We can see Kant as thinking that he has reconciled any potential conflict between the definition of Right as enforceable and the definition of Right as the use of freedom in accordance with universal law by the use of the straightforward logic, and that he is capping this reconciliation by the definition of strict Right. But by the latter he is not introducing a new category of Right or a subset of the original category of Right: all genuine Right is strict Right according to Kant's initial definition.

At this point in Kant's series of definitions, it might be objected that Kant is overlooking his own longstanding distinction between logical and real relations,[46] and that he needs to show that it is really possible for a use of coercion, which considered in itself is always an abridgement of someone's freedom, that of the person coerced, to preserve freedom in accordance with a universal law, which would seem to have to include the freedom of everyone involved, the would-be perpetrator of a violation of Right as well as the would-be victim. Although Kant does not supply such an argument, this can be done by supposing that if the laws and potential punishments for their violation in any actual state are public and known, the would-be perpetrator of a crime has a free choice between committing his crime and suffering the potential consequences of it, or not so choosing, and thus always has the option of a free choice to preserve his own freedom in a way that the would-be victim of his crime would not. That is, under a system of public laws there is always a way to preserve freedom in accordance with universal law, and when someone freely chooses to break a law, he has in fact freely chosen to do that and to risk the associated punishment. A system of enforcement to preserve freedom can in fact preserve freedom.[47]

---

[45] The twentieth-century conception of analyticity was something like whatever could be derived from a definition by logical means alone. W.V.O. Quine's famous attack upon analyticity in "Two Dogmas of Empiricism" (1951, reprinted in Quine 1953) was not directed against the assumption that logical principles could be well defined, but rather that definitions could be well defined. As we are about to see, Kant himself held that philosophical arguments could not be based on definitions and logic alone, but the use of any definition itself has to be justified.

[46] See his 1763 essay "Attempt to Introduce the Concept of Negative Magnitudes in Philosophy," 2:165–204, translated in Kant (1992, pp. 203–41).

[47] Here is where we could say that there is a need for a "postulate" or "construction" of the concept of Right, to show that in the real world there always is a solution to any potential conflict between the freedom of multiple persons. Kant hints at the need to demonstrate that there is in fact always some solution to any potential collision of uses of freedom on which the maximal yet equal freedom of all can be preserved when he says that "The law of a reciprocal coercion necessarily in accord with the freedom of everyone under the principle of universal freedom is, as it were, the **construction** of that concept [of Right], that is, the presentation of it in pure intuition *a priori*, by analogy with presenting the possibility of bodies moving freely under the law of the **equality of action and reaction**" (DR, Introduction, section E, 6:232). The demonstration that to a free action on the part of one person that would nonreciprocally hinder the freedom of another there is always an alternative that preserves the freedom of each does not seem quite like a construction

The Moral Foundation of Right

But the main point that I want to make here is that in Kant's view conclusive philosophical arguments can never be based on definitions alone.[48] They need some external or additional ground to prove that the definition has "objective reality," or really applies to something actual, in the first place. This is a foundation of Kant's "critical" philosophy, and Kant makes this point in many ways and applies it in many cases. He states the general principle at the beginning of the central argument of the *Critique of Pure Reason*, the "Transcendental Deduction" of the "Pure Concepts of the Understanding": concepts that are not derived directly from experience, which categories that are supposed to hold necessarily and universally can never be, must be shown not to be merely "usurped," such as concepts like "fortune" and "fate," which we can define but cannot show that we have any right to use (A 84/B 117). His famous critique of the ontological argument is nothing other than an argument that we cannot derive the existence of God from a mere definition of the concept of God, but must instead have some antecedent reason to believe that such a concept applies to something real in the first place. Or, as Kant's defender J.G. Schulze explained,

> Let one place just so many marks in the concept of a subject that the predicate, which he wishes to prove of the subject, can be derived from its concept through the mere principle of contradiction. This trick does not help him at all. For the *Critique* [*of Pure Reason*] grants to him without dispute this kind of analytic judgment. Then, however, it takes the concept of the subject itself into consideration, and it asks: how did it come about that you have placed so many different marks in this concept that it already contains synthetic propositions. First prove the objective reality of your concept, i.e., first prove that any one of its marks really belongs to a possible object, and then, when you have done that, prove that the other marks belong to the same thing that the first one belongs to.[49]

In other words, no informative, in Kant's usage "synthetic" propositions, are ever proven from definitions alone. Any definition must be shown to have "objective reality," or actually to apply to some existing object; only then will whatever follows from the definition by logical rules also be shown to have objective reality. Or, in the normative case, it must first be shown that a definition really does state an obligation for us, and only then will whatever follows from the definition also turn out to apply. Show that the definition of

---

in mathematics or physics, but some such proof that there is always a possibility of reciprocal freedom seems to be required.
[48] See also Gregor (1963, p. 35).
[49] J.G. Schulze, Review of the Second Volume of the *Philosophisches Magazin*, translated in Allison (1973, p. 175). The importance of this passage was first pointed out by Lewis White Beck in 1955; see Beck (1965, pp. 83–4).

Right actually applies to us, or is actually normative for us, and then the further inference that Right is strict Right, that coercion may be used to enforce it, will also apply to us. But definitions alone will never show that any norms apply to us.

Thus Kant's definitions of Right and of the Universal Principle of Right in the Introduction to the Doctrine of Right do not constitute a premise from which whatever follows can be shown to bind us. They merely define a concept – Right – that must still be shown to express a binding obligation for us. Kant is perfectly well aware of this methodological point, his own fundamental methodological point, and so, just as in the *Groundwork* he added an "ostensive" proof of the moral law with the assertion of the fact that our nature marks us out as persons and ends in ourselves to the merely "apagogic" argument for the first formulation of the categorical imperative, so in the Introduction to the Doctrine of Right does he follow the initial definition of Right with the justifying *ground* for that definition: the "innate right" to freedom that each of us possesses in virtue of the humanity in each of us, or the obligation that each of us has to treat the humanity in all of us as an end and never merely as a means.

Kant takes this crucial step under the bland title of a general "Division of Rights." The first division is the familiar one between "natural Right," "which rests only on *a priori* principles," and "positive Right," "which proceeds from the will of a legislator," that is, is the legislation in some actual state. It goes without saying by this point in Kant's exposition that the former is to be the moral standard for the latter. The moral character of rights, thus collectively of Right, is then made explicit in Kant's second and "highest division":

> The highest division of rights, as (moral) **capacities** for putting others under obligation (i.e., as a lawful basis, *titulum*, for doing so), is the division into **innate** and **acquired** Right. An innate right is that which belongs to everyone by nature, independently of any act that would establish a right; an acquired right is that for which such act is required. (DR, Introduction, Division of the Doctrine of Right, 6:237)

Kant's use of the term "nature" here is telling: as in Kant's argument in the *Groundwork* that humanity whether in one's own person or that of any other is the ground of a possible categorical imperative, it signals the factual basis for the application of a moral concept, in this case the concept of innate right, to us. Kant then explains: "**Freedom** (independence from being constrained by another's choice), insofar as it can coexist with the freedom of every other in accordance with a universal law, is the only original right belonging to every human being by virtue of his humanity" (6:237). Everyone has a right to freedom in virtue of his humanity, that is, his ability set his own ends; everyone has such a right because humanity and thus freedom is the end in itself, thus we have an *obligation* to treat it always as an end and never merely as a means, and *right is the correlative of obligation*. If I have some obligation to you, then you have a right to my fulfillment of that obligation; if I have an obligation to everyone, then everyone has a right to my fulfillment of that obligation. Since humanity is freedom, the freedom to set our own ends, the obligation that we each have to the humanity in all, in our own person and that of every other, as the sole end in itself, entails a correlative right of all to as much freedom as is conjointly possible for everyone.[50] This is the moral foundation of Kant's doctrine of Right, the something "given" that makes the mere definition of Right applicable to and normative for us. The innate right to freedom is grounded in our fundamental obligation to treat the freedom of all as an end and never merely as a means, and is in turn the ground of the Universal Principle of Right, just as the humanity in us all is the ground of the imperative always to act only on universalizable maxims. Kant has followed his own methodology: first the analysis of the concept of Right, then the proof that this concept has objective reality.[51]

Kant spells out what is contained in the concept of innate right and thus what is our moral obligation in the case of Right in terms of three entitlements.[52] Kant says that these are "not really distinct from" the concept of innate right, "as if they were members of the division of some higher concept of Right" (as say *Australopithecus* and modern *Homo sapiens* might be species of some higher genus of hominids); they are simply the marks of this concept, its predicates; perhaps the importance of this remark is that the concept cannot be satisfied if just one of its entitlements is observed, while the genus of hominids still exists

---

[50] In spite of other differences, John Stuart Mill did not differ from Kant on this point: "The only freedom which deserves the name, is that of pursuing our own good in our own way, so long as we do not attempt to deprive others of theirs, or impede their efforts to obtain it. . . . Though this doctrine is anything but new, and, to some persons, may have the air of a truism, there is no doctrine which stands more opposed to the general tendency of existing opinion and action" (Mill 1977, p. 226).

[51] My argument is that just as in the *Groundwork* the Formula of Humanity as an End in Itself expresses the "ground of a possible categorical imperative" including the Formula of Universal Law, so in the *Doctrine of Right* the obligation that we have toward the inborn freedom of each grounds the Right of all. It is on this point that my approach differs from that of Gregor, who thought that the Formula of Humanity follows from the Formula of Universal Law (Gregor 1963, p. 39), and Pauer-Studer, who thinks that the Formula of Humanity follows from the Formula of the Realm (or Empire) of Ends, although her conclusion in fact shows the opposite (Pauer-Studer 2016, pp. 146, 173).

[52] Kant's term is "*Befügnisse*," which Mary Gregor translates as "authorizations" but John Ladd as "entitlements." Mulholland (1990) translates the term as "titles," which sounds too much like a term from real estate law, but has a good discussion of innate right at pp. 220–7; see also Ripstein (2009, pp. 40–52), and Pinzani (2021, pp. 83–7).

even if only one species, namely, modern humans, survives. Innate Right demands that all of the entitlements always be satisfied. These entitlements are: "innate **equality**, that is, independence from being bound by others to more than one can in turn bind them, hence a human being's quality of being **his own master** (*sui iuris*)," that is, the right to deal with others always from a position of equality; "being a human being **beyond reproach** (*iusti*), since before he performs any act affecting rights he has done no wrong to anyone," that is, the right to continue to enjoy one's equal freedom with others as long as one has not by one's own act brought down any limitation of freedom upon oneself;[53] and third, "being authorized to do to others anything that does not in itself diminish what is theirs," that is, their freedom, "so long as they do not want to accept it – such things as merely communicating [one's] thoughts to them, whether what [one] says is true and sincere or untrue and insincere (*veriloquium aut falsiloquium*); for it is" – that is, *as long as it is* – "entirely up to them whether they want to believe him or not" (6:237–8).

The entitlements are forms of freedom of action. Everyone has as much right to freedom as everyone else, so no one is naturally inferior to any other in this regard. Thus no one has an innate right to limit or destroy the freedom of another unless the other has brought that on himself by his own action. And because everyone has an innate right to freedom, no one has the right to manipulate or defraud others, because manipulation and fraud are deprivations of freedom, but as long as one leaves others free to make their up their own minds what to believe, say, or do, one can oneself believe, say, or do whatever one wants.[54] For Kant this is the basis as well as the limit not only for free speech but also for freedom of religion, as the freedom to believe whatever one wants about religious matters, for belief by itself cannot limit the freedom of any other; as the freedom to say what one wants about religious matters, as long as one is leaving others free to believe and say what they want, not for example brainwashing them as in a cult; and as the freedom to practice religion as one believes

---

[53] This is not the merely procedural principle of burden of proof that an accused person is innocent, that is, to be *adjudged* innocent, as long as he is not proven guilty; it is the substantive principle that one *is* innocent and therefore entitled to continue to enjoy one's innate right of freedom unless one *is* guilty of something.

[54] Kant had not quite reached this position in *Naturrecht Feyerabend*. There he said that a right to "declare one's mind" is part of innate right, that an intentional falsehood to another's disadvantage is a mendacious falsehood and presumably properly punishable at law, but that "every untruth even about unimportant matters" is mendacious and justifies others in discrediting the liar even if not taking him to law (L-NR, 27:1340). His position in the *Doctrine of Right* is that only an intentional falsehood that injures the freedom of another is a violation of strict Right and therefore legally preventable or punishable, while any other lie is only a violation of ethical duty to oneself (DV, §9, 6:429–31). He does not mention the intermediate position that the latter sort of lie is a wrong to the other that may be punished, although not at law but by public shaming.

best, as long as one's practice is not interfering with the freedom of others to practice religion, or anything else, as they want. This last element of freedom of religion is the basis for the proviso in Kant's defense of the separation of church of state, as in every other defense from the days of Roger Williams and John Locke, that "A state has only a **negative** right to prevent public teachers [of religion] from exercising an influence on the **visible** commonwealth that might be prejudicial to the public peace" (DR, General Remark C, 6:327).[55]

As we have just seen, Kant divides Right into the two classes, innate and acquired Right. The latter is in turn divided into several possible acquired rights, such as the rights to possess land, to enter into contracts with other persons for particular actions, and to enter into long-term relationships with other persons that are defined and to that extent protected by law such as marriage, parenthood, and employment (rights to things, to persons, and to persons as akin to things).[56] There is just the one innate Right to freedom, although that can be analyzed into its three entitlements which, however, remain very general, while there are multiple species of acquired rights, which have been developed in great detail by all systems of law. For that reason Kant can say that innate Right has been adequately discussed in the "prolegomena and division of the Doctrine of Right" and that the two main sections of the following book can be reserved for expounding the complex of acquired rights and then "Public Right," that is, the rights – and responsibilities – connected with the state, as the instrument for the enforcement of rights through its positive legislation and its juridical and penal institutions. But it would be a mistake to infer from this organizational choice that the public laws and institutions are necessary to define and enforce only acquired right, because the elements of innate Right need specification and enforcement in the actual circumstances of human life just as much as acquired rights do.[57] For example, although we are all innately entitled to freedom of

---

[55] For more on Kant's view on freedom of religion, see Guyer (2020b) and (2022b).

[56] Some reviewers thought that this last class of rights was a "new phenomenon in the juridical heavens" (Bouterwek 1797, p. 91), and it might seem as if Kant advocated treating some people as things, or "objectifying" them. But Kant is doing precisely the opposite, arguing that even in long-term relationships in which one person has an enduring right of control over another, like a relationship to a thing, the other is *still* a person and has to be treated as such. Thus wives or servants are *not* and cannot be *treated* as mere things. Kant makes this clear in his response to Bouterwek: the right that he is discussing is "to make direct use of a person **as of a thing**, as a means to my end, but still without infringing upon his personality . . . as the condition under which such use is legitimate" (DR, Appendix, 6:359).

[57] Ripstein (2009, p. 23) suggests that it is only "the requirements of private right – the security of possession, clear boundaries between 'mine and thine,' and the acquisition of property – that cannot be satisfied without a public authority entitled to make, apply and enforce laws." No: public authority is also needed to define the boundaries of free speech, of separation of church and state, what counts as equality before the law, and so on. In the United States, much Supreme Court jurisprudence concerns precisely such issues.

speech, we may still need law to specify that it is permissible to yell "Fire!" in the middle of a wide-open field but not in a crowded theater – or that screaming "You won't have a country unless you fight for it!" to an armed horde is not permitted speech but incitement to riot that should be punished.

Kant's word "prolegomena" might suggest a mere preface rather than a *foundation*, but the innate Right to freedom is the foundation of acquired Right. The right to do anything that leaves others equally free is the basis of the right to acquire property or enter into short- or long-term agreements with others as long as so doing leaves everyone affected as free as everyone else. What Kant does in his treatment of acquired Right is to show how property can be acquired or contracts made or long-term relationships managed in ways that leave everyone involved with their innate Right to freedom. For example, the acquisition and possession of property requires an "omnilateral" rather than a "unilateral will"; that is, it must be possible for everyone affected to agree freely to a system of property rights, because the freedom of each to use land or objects is affected by the property rights of others (DR, §8, 6:255–6). The conditions for acquired rights are grounded in the innate Right to freedom, which is in turn grounded in our shared humanity, and the basic categories of acquired Right could not be denied without denying the innate Right to freedom itself.[58] This is not to confuse innate and acquired Right, for acquired rights require the consent of others to one's particular claims (explicit consent in the case of contracts or marriages, for example, perhaps tacit consents in relation to some aspects of property rights, and innate Right requires no such consent. But all have an innate Right to demand the consent of others under appropriate conditions, and all have a moral obligation not to withhold consent under appropriate conditions. That is the sense in which the right to acquire acquired rights is part of everyone's innate Right to freedom grounded in the moral obligation of all to respect the humanity in each.

In fact, not only did every author of the period include the right to acquire property on their lists of innate rights, but in the *Naturrecht Feyerabend* lectures Kant did so too. There Kant offers the vague definition of "original natural right" that it is "the right of a human being insofar as it rests merely on inner

---

[58] Ripstein (2009) says more vaguely that "innate right leads to private right" (p. 13), and somewhat more clearly that "By making the innate right to freedom the basis for any further rights, Kant imposes an extreme demand for unity on his account of political justice" (p. 31). Gregor (1963, p. 50) says more clearly yet that "the title to acquire objects of choice is contained in the inherent right to freedom." Mulholland (1990) says correctly that "innate right forms the basis for Kant on human rights generally" (p. 200) and determines "that if it is possible for a person to acquire exclusive use of an external object," the basic form of private Right, "and this exclusive use can coexist with everyone's freedom in accordance with a universal law, then he has the right to the external object" (p. 211).

laws" (L-NR, 27:1338), which tells us that it does not depend on any external legislation or juridical act, such as making a contract, thus it does not arise from any social contract and obtains in *status naturalis* as well as *civilis*. The auditors had to fill in from what Kant had previously said that freedom is the end and reason merely the means; thus, innate Right must be the right to every form of freedom that can coexist with the equal freedom of others. Kant then follows Achenwall and other writers of the time by simply listing a number of *jura connata*, or inborn rights. The list that Kant offers is

(1) "No one does wrong to another if he performs actions that concern himself alone" (27:1338); such actions are exercises of one's innate right to freedom that by definition do not interfere with the freedom of others.
(2) "All are equal to each other, not in understanding, powers, but in right," so "Inequality of right must originate through *factum juridicum*" or some particular deed (27:1338–9).
(3) "*Libertas*: Before *factum juridicum* I infringe on no one and thus also no one can limit my freedom."
(4) "The right to a good reputation."
(5) "A *jus connatum* to acquire things" (27:1339).
(and (6), the right to declare one's mind, already mentioned).

Among these (2) corresponds to the first entitlement that he lists in his mature analysis of innate right, (3) and (4) correspond to the second entitlement in that list, and (1) is the basis of the third entitlement of innate right, the right to do anything to others that one wants as long as it does not limit their freedom. However, although (5), the inborn right to acquire things, is missing from Kant's later analysis of innate right, it should be included on the grounds that, first, acquiring and possessing property does not limit the freedom of that which is possessed, for example land or cattle, for those things possess no freedom to be limited, and, second, does not unequally limit the freedom of other human beings as long as they could freely agree to the acquisition or possession. In the *Doctrine of Right* Kant makes the first of these conditions more explicit than the second, emphasizing in its "Postulate of practical reason with regard to rights" that "freedom would be depriving itself of the use of its choice with regard to an object of choice by putting **usable** objects" – that do *not* have any will and thus any possibility of freedom of their own – "beyond any possibility of being **used**" (DR, §6, 6:250). But in the lectures Kant makes both conditions for the exercise of the innate right to acquire rights explicit, although in reverse order to what I have listed:

> *A natura* everyone is *sui juris* [his own master], but not also [master of] things for they are not innate to him. Before *factum juridicum* I do not have

a positive right to a thing. [One] does have a negative right of nature because he cannot do wrong to a thing. If he cuts down a tree then he already has an affirmative right that has first occurred by means of *factum juridicum*. (L-NR, 27:1339)

It is possible to acquire rights to things, for example, a tree that one has cut down, because such things have no will and hence no possibility of freedom of their own (at least on Kant's view of such things as trees). But that is only a necessary condition of the rightful acquisition of property, what Kant calls a negative right; for a sufficient condition for rightful acquisition, or what Kant calls an affirmative right, the consent of others, at least their possible consent, is required – there has to be some form of agreement that one had a right to cut down that tree in the first place. This is what Kant implies by his claim that a "*factum juridicum*" must have *first* occurred, although "*factum juridicum*" has to be understood broadly here, as referring not just to a particular act, such as a contract with the proprietor of a Christmas tree farm that creates the right to cut down one of his trees at a specified price, but also as referring more generally to a tacit or explicit but in either case free acceptance of a scheme of property rights. For it to be possible for all concerned to accept any such scheme freely it would presumably be necessary for each to regard it as sufficiently in their own interest to do so, or for the scheme to reach some standard of fairness.[59] The point is that the right to acquire acquired rights is itself part of innate Right. Kant had also made this explicit in his preliminary sketches of the *Doctrine of Right*: "we have an innate right to acquire all that we are able to use, though only insofar as it agrees with that condition of the outer unity of powers of choice" (Kant 1900—, 23:220; Kant 2016, p. 258) – namely, the possible coexistence of the freedom of all, or, as Kant calls it here, "the idea of a united will."[60]

Kant's doctrine of Right, beginning with innate Right as the basis for all acquired Right, is founded on our obligation to treat the humanity of all as an end in itself, indeed the sole end in itself. Since Kant makes it clear in the seminal works of 1784–85, the *Groundwork* but also the lectures on natural right, that this is the foundation of morality in general, this should make it clear that Kant's doctrine of Right is grounded on the fundamental principle of morality and is an integral part of his moral philosophy.

I will now conclude this Element by pointing to several features of Kant's political theory that make sense only if we assume that Right, or the establishment and maintenance of a condition of Right through the legislative, juridical, and penal institutions of the state, is a moral obligation, not a mere matter of prudence.

---

[59] See Guyer (2000, chapters 7 and 8).
[60] This text is cited, although not quoted, at Gregor (1963, p. 50n2).

4 Political Morality

Three points in Kant's treatment of the state – what he calls "Public Right," what we might call political philosophy proper – make sense only if Right is founded on the fundamental principle of morality, not mere prudence. First, when human beings find that they cannot avoid contact with each other – a circumstance that almost always obtains, stories about castaways and human children brought up by wolves notwithstanding – they are under an obligation to enter into a state, the "civil condition," with each other, that is, a condition in which the component elements of innate Right and a system of acquired rights are made determinate by legislation and secured by the juridical and penal institutions of a state. Although it is in fact usually prudent for people to be part of such a state, perhaps always, as Hobbes had argued, some might think that in some circumstances they might be better off without it – but as a moral duty, the duty to be part of a state nevertheless applies to them. Second, although Kant believes that actual states have typically arisen in circumstances of violence and conflict (TPP, 8:363, 365; DV, §52, 6:339) out of which rulers have emerged because of contingent factors such as their strength or luck, those who find themselves in positions of power have an obligation to transform their states into just ones – in Kant's view, republics in which laws are made by a legislature that represents the sovereignty of the people and in which the executive who enforces laws, as applied by a judiciary, is merely an agent of that legislature. This obligation can only arise from morality itself, not from prudence as it might for a Machiavellian prince. And third, citizens of a republic, or even subjects of a pre-republican state that has not yet realized the ideal of republican form, have a moral duty to avoid anarchy and maintain the existence of the state, although that must be accompanied with their innate right to freedom in the form of the freedom of speech, pen, and press necessary to bring injustices to the attention of their rulers and to petition for reform. All three of these duties have the unremitting form of moral obligation, and cannot be understood as mere counsels of prudence.

4.1 The Moral Duty to Enter a State

(i) The first of these moral duties is the duty to become part of a state. Kant explicates this obligation in §§41 and 42 of the Doctrine of Right, which effect the transition between its two main sections on "Private Right" and "Public Right."[61] Kant begins the transition with a restatement of his definition of Right,

---

[61] The original editions of the *Rechtslehre*, the *Akademie* edition, and Gregor's translation all place these sections at the end of Private Right. Ludwig and following him Ladd in the second edition of his translation reposition these two sections to the opening of Public Right. But this switch

although after the detailed exposition of the particular ways in which freedom is to be preserved in innate Right and the acquired rights to property, contract, and relationships that he has offered in Private Right, he now can speak of rights instead of speaking directly of freedom: "The rightful condition [*Das rechtliche Zustand*] is that relation of human beings among one another that contains the conditions under which alone everyone is able to **participate** in his rights, and the formal condition under which this is possible in accordance with the idea of a will giving laws for everyone is called public justice [*Gerechtigkeit*]" (DR, §41, 6:305–6). In other words, Right obtains when everyone can enjoy the freedom embodied in their innate and acquired rights, as required by morality, and public Right is the "formal condition" of this enjoyment, what makes it determinate and secure. Kant stresses that public Right serves to realize private Right (although as we saw innate Right also needs to be made determinate and secure): it "contains no further or other duties of human beings among themselves than can be conceived in the former state"; "the matter of private Right is the same in both. The laws of the condition of public Right, therefore, have to do only with the rightful form of their association (constitution), in view of which these laws must necessarily be conceived as public" (6:306). Since the content of innate and private Right flows from the moral imperative to realize the greatest possible freedom of each to the extent consistent with the same freedom for all, and public Right has no purpose except to realize innate and private Right, its justification and necessity are also moral in origin.

Kant defines a "rightful condition" more fully as comprising "**protective justice** (*iustitita tutatrix*)," "**justice in acquiring from one another**" (*iustitia commutativa*)," and "**distributive justice** (*iustitia distributiva*)" (6:306).[62] The first of these presumably means the protection of rights and possessions that people already have, the second a requirement of fairness in transfers, and the third Kant has defined as "legitimacy of possession, not the way it would be judged **in itself** by the private will of each (in the state of nature), but the way it would be judged before a **court** in a condition brought about by the united will of all" (DR, §39, 6:302). In other words, distributive justice obtains when a system of rights, that, is conditions for the exercise of innate Right and the acquisition of the various forms of acquired rights, could be freely agreed to by all, which could presumably happen only if the system can be perceived as adequately in the interest of each.[63] But distributive justice, Kant also argues,

---

makes no difference between their interpretations; either way these two sections constitute the transition from Private to Public Right.

[62] On these terms see Byrd and Hruschka (2010, pp. 71–6).

[63] Perhaps, as suggested by John Rawls's "difference principle," which we might think of as his version of the principle of distributive justice, as adequately in the interest of all and better for the

can obtain only in a civil condition (*status civilis*) as opposed to the state of nature (*status naturalis*): the civil condition is defined by the existence of laws that "determine," that is, make fully determinate, "what conduct is intrinsically **right**, in terms of its form" and "what [objects] are capable of being covered externally by laws, in terms of their matter," thus which together define which rights people have with regard to which sorts of objects, and of courts that can "give the decision in a particular case in accordance with the given law under which it falls," in other words, which can determine precisely how the relevant laws apply to particular circumstances (§41, 6:306). In his initial definition of distributive justice, while also suggesting that distributive justice can only obtain in a civil condition, Kant also attempts to clarify the distinction between distributive justice and the other two forms of justice by arguing that in the state of nature people have rights only against each other, presumably as a product of innate Right plus particular agreements about matters of private Right that they have made, but only in the civil condition do they actually have rights against things (§39, 6:303), presumably meaning by this that only under the rule of law and courts can people have rights to possessions that must be recognized by anyone even without personal agreements between the holder of such rights and others, such as passers-by who might trespass on their land. Surprisingly, Kant makes no mention in these passages of the need for an executive authority in the civil condition to *enforce* the application of the laws (made by a legislature) to particular cases (as determined by courts), when in a political theory such as Hobbes's the role of the executive is really the raison d'etre for the state and the main motivation for people leaving the state of nature to enter into the civil condition.

Later Kant certainly will recognize the role of the executive as well as the legislature and judiciary:

> Every state contains three *powers* [*Gewalten*] within it, that is, the general united will consists of three persons (*trias politica*): the **sovereign power** (sovereignty) [*Herrschergewalt* (*Souveränität*)] in the person of the legislator; the **executive power** [*vollziehende Gewalt*] in the person of the ruler [*Regierers*] (in conformity to law); and the **judicial power** (to award to each what is his in accordance with the law) in the person of the judge (*potestas legislatoria, rectoria et iudiciaria*).

Kant analogizes the three persons of the state to the three steps in a "practical syllogism," "the major premise, which contains the **law** of that will; the minor

---

least well-off than any other scheme available in the relevant actual circumstances. See Rawls (1999, chapter II, §§11–13, and chapter V, §§41–3, pp. 52–73 and 228–51), as well as Rawls (2001, §§14–19, pp. 50–72).

premise, which contains the **command** to behave in accordance with the law, that is, the principle of subsumption under the law; and the conclusion, which contains the **verdict** (sentence), what is laid down as right in the case at hand" (§45, 6:313). One might have thought that the law that functions as the major premise of this syllogism *is* a command to behave in a certain way, and the analogy might better have been between the law promulgated by a legislature as the major premise, the decision of a court that a particular action falls under that law as the minor premise, and the action of the executive to enforce the ruling of the court as the conclusion.[64] Be that as it may, Kant's omission of the role of the executive in his initial definitions of the civil condition is striking. Perhaps this is just an expository failing on Kant's part, or perhaps it is a subtle way of preparing the ground for the argument that he will subsequently make that the executive is merely an agent of the legislature that has the role of enforcing laws but most decidedly *not* making the laws *or* interpreting them, the functions of the legislature and judiciary respectively (§49, 6:316–17). His use of the term *Herrscher* to characterize the role of the legislature and mere *Regierer*, which could also be translated as "regent," to characterize the role of the executive, might also be part of that diminution of the role of the executive. Kant was firm on that point, but may have felt that he had to express it subtly and cautiously in the autocratic Prussia of his time, in which as a professor he had been a public employee.[65]

The main point here is that Kant recognizes a *moral* permission and indeed obligation to establish and enter into the civil condition. This is clear from the "postulate of public Right" with which he begins the second transitional section between private and public Right:[66] "From private Right in the state of nature there proceeds the postulate of public Right: when you cannot avoid living side by side with all others, you ought to leave the state of nature and proceed with them into a rightful condition, that is, a condition of distributive justice" (DR, §42, 6:307), which is in turn, as Kant had just argued, the civil condition – the state. You ought to enter the state. Using his favorite terminology, Kant continues that "The ground of this postulate can be explicated analytically from the concept of **right** in external relations, in contrast with **violence** (*violentia*)." The right as well as the obligation to be part of a state follows analytically from

---

[64] Most commentators on Kant's analogies between the three powers of government and the three steps in a syllogism are content with Kant's explication of it; for example, Ripstein (2009, p. 174), and Byrd and Hrushka (2010, pp. 157–61). I think that the modification proposed here makes the main relation between the executive and the judiciary clearer.

[65] On "Kant and Prussian Politics," see Beiser (1992, pp. 48–53).

[66] As we saw, there had also been a "postulate of practical reason with regard to [private] rights" (DR, §6, 6:250), which had established the moral permissibility of and conditions for the acquisition of property, although only incompletely.

the concept of right itself because, as we saw, the right to coercive enforcement of one's rights and indeed the obligation to coercively enforce rights follows analytically from the concept of right itself, and the state is the instrument of such coercion, which can itself be established by coercion. But, as we also saw, the *concept* of right by itself does not establish our obligations; rather, rights follow from our obligation toward persons as ends in themselves. Rights are the means by which to fulfill our fundamental moral obligation to preserve freedom in our interactions with each other. So if the concept of Right entails the possibility and necessity of coercive enforcement, and the state or civil condition is the means for realizing Right, as Kant's analogy with the practical syllogism expresses, then the right and the obligation to enter into the civil condition follows from the fundamental principle of morals itself. Each person has the obligation to do so, and the right against others that they do so.

Kant's next paragraph might mislead a reader into thinking that for Kant the necessity of the state is after all grounded in mere prudence rather than in morality, in which case it would be only a relative necessity, contingent upon particular circumstances such as whom one encounters and how strong they actually are. Kant says that

> No one is bound to refrain from encroaching on what another possesses if the other gives him no equal assurance that he will observe the same constraint toward him. No one, therefore, need wait until he has learned by bitter experience of the other's contrary disposition; for what should bind him to wait until he has suffered a loss before he becomes prudent, when he can quite well perceive within himself the inclination of human beings generally to lord it over others as their master (not to recognize the superiority of the rights of others when they feel superior to them in strength or cunning)? (DR, §42, 6:307)

Kant uses the word "prudent" (*klug*) here, so this sounds like a counsel of prudence, and no doubt it *is* a counsel of prudence: if you think that others around you will not respect your personal freedom and possessions and have the strength to take them from you, then it certainly is prudent to seek the protection of a state against them. But Kant immediately adds that one is *entitled* (*befugt*) "to use coercion against someone who already, by his nature, threatens him with coercion." Here Kant is using the terminology of his original explication of the innate Right to freedom. And as we are entitled to coercive enforcement of our rights, the use of coercion through the instrument of the state is just the form that our permissible use of coercion against the threat of coercion takes. Since that was authorized as a hindrance to the hindrance of freedom, and that is authorized by the moral value of freedom itself, so is membership in a state not merely prudent but an enforceable right authorized by morality.

Kant continues in a moral tone in the final paragraph of §42:

> Given the intention to be and remain in this state of externally lawless freedom, men do **one another** no wrong at all when they feud among themselves; for what holds for one in holds also in turn for the other, as if by mutual consent (*uti partes de iure suo disponunt, ita ius ist*); but in general they do what is unjust in the highest degree by willing to remain in a condition that is not rightful, i.e., in which no one is secure in what is his against violence. (DR, §42, 6:307–8)

That is, while it is prudent to take steps, even proactively, against others who will not assure one of one's rights, it is wrong for everyone involved to remain in such a state of hostility; Right requires that everyone leave such a state and enter into the civil condition.

Kant's use of "ought" (*sollst*) in the statement of the postulate of public right is in the second person, addressed to each of us in the same verbal form in which any moral obligation can be stated. So we each have an obligation to be part of a state governed by law, the civil condition, if we cannot simply avoid contact with other persons, which we cannot avoid in the actual conditions of human existence. But Kant's talk of an entitlement to threaten the other with coercion against his own potential coercion implies a right to compel the other to enter into the civil condition along with oneself. In Kant's view, this follows from the nature of a right, as including the right to enforcement, and from the moral fact that we *have* a right to our freedom. This is not just prudence.

One of the most astute reviewers of Kant's *Rechtslehre* objected to Kant's view that we have a right to compel others to join in a state with oneself. Ludwig Heinrich Jakob, to whose book on Moses Mendelssohn's *Morgenstunden* ("Morning Lessons," 1785) Kant had earlier contributed a preface,[67] wrote that

> The obligation not to injure the rights of others is self-evident. Everyone is permitted to provide for the security of his own [property], but only through rightful means. The suspicion that another might attack us cannot justify us in anything except strengthening our own power and thereby influencing him with fear, but never in first initiating hostility, as [Kant] will have it. – That it is the nature of the human being already to threaten the other with his coercion, is an empirical proposition that permits infinite exceptions, and even when it is the case nothing follows from it except that everyone must make an effort to provide his well-intentioned assistance against such a hostile being; but he is never permitted to overstep the command not to injure the freedom of others if his own is not first injured. It is possible in itself to secure my rights against hostile attacks through well-intentioned union

---

[67] "*Einige Bemerkungen zu L.H. Jakob's Prüfung der Mendelssohn'schen Morgenstunden*," 8:140–55, translated in Kant (2007, pp. 178–81). For Mendelssohn's *Morgenstunden* ("Morning Hours" or "Lessons"), see Mendelssohn (2011) and (2012).

with others who find an interest in this union. .... However this is possible without my forcing [hostile others] into joining a civil condition with me.[68]

Like every other author of the time, including Achenwall, Jakob recognized that any right, in Achenwall's case the right to self-preservation and therefore to the means to it, includes the means to realize that right. Jakob though that means to protect one's rights and possessions from hostile attackers were justified, including the right to voluntary association with like-minded others for this purpose. But he did not see how this gives anyone a positive right to force others to enter into a state with him.

> The proposition, therefore, which constitutes a chief foundation of the entire Kantian natural right, and with that so many other propositions, among them also that of an unconditional civil obedience, is namely that all genuine right first becomes possible through the state, or that the civil condition is the only one conceivable in which each can participate in his rights, this reviewer holds to be unproven, together with its numerous and diverse consequences.[69]

However, Jakob may not have fully understood Kant's recognition that the threat of hostility is itself a form of coercion that justifies counter-coercion, not as a matter of mere prudence but as a matter of right, thus that coercing others into joining a state with one is coercion intended to hinder coercion, not unprovoked coercion as he thinks it would be.

Another earlier reviewer, Friedrich Bouterwek, might also have failed to understand the full import of Kant's justification of coercion. He applauded Kant's general principle that "in accordance with the idea of universal freedom (limited only by the moral law) I cannot treat a person as a thing [*Sache*], for that would exclude a being from the idea of universal freedom who is yet comprehended under this idea" – indeed, he captures in this formulation Kant's underlying idea that there is a logical contradiction in treating someone who has a will of his own as if he does not. And he has no objection to Kant's specific view that rightful "Coercion is nothing but hindering a hindrance of freedom." However, he takes from this only a negative concept of Right, that "the juridical concept of Right only **limits** the freedom of the other, insofar as this cannot coexist with the freedom of all; but it does not describe any law through which the other can be obligated to *do* something."[70] However, this does not recognize that for Kant rights and obligations are always correlative: if I have the right that you not do something, then you have an obligation not to do it and I have the right to enforce that obligation; and if the only way to hinder your coercive threat to my right is itself a form of coercion, as forcing you to join with me in

---

[68] Jakob (1797, p. 68; my translation).   [69] Jakob (1797, p. 69; my translation).
[70] Bouterwek (1797, p. 88; my translation).

a civil condition would be, then I have a right to that coercion, as hindering a hindrance to my freedom. Kant would not accept Bouterwek's objection, although in his replies to Bouterwek's review, in an Appendix added to the second edition of the *Rechtslehre* (DR, 6:356–72), he replies not to this point but to a different objection, namely, Bouterwek's objection to his own rejection of a right to rebellion. We will come back to that issue shortly; for now we can conclude that, whatever the merits of his argument, Kant himself certainly thought that all who cannot avoid coming into contact with each other have an obligation to enter into the civil condition with each other and therefore that any of them have the right to enforce this obligation, that is, to force others to enter into a state with them – or, if the state already exists, as in human history it usually does, to continue to maintain that state along with them. Such a right can only be grounded in moral obligation.

4.2 The Moral Obligation of Rulers

Kant also argues that those in positions of power in their states have a duty to rule in accordance with the idea of Right. This can only be a moral duty, in fact an ethical duty, since it cannot be imposed on those who rule the state by anyone other than themselves. Unlike Machiavelli, Kant does not argue that it is in the self-interest of rulers to rule with the mere appearance of morality.

Kant holds that only a republican government can truly make innate and acquired right determinate and secure, in his terms deliver distributive justice. Republican government is defined along two axes, which we might define, again in Kantian fashion, formally and materially. Formally, or structurally, republican government is distinguished by the distribution of the three *functions* of government, legislation, adjudication, and enforcement, among three different *persons*, a legislature, a judiciary, and an executive. These may be natural or artificial persons (DR, §49, 6:316), that is, single persons or groups. It is crucial that these three functions be divided among different persons so that those who have the power to adjudicate cases under the law or enforce those judgments will not have had the opportunity to make the laws in their own favor from the outset. Kant states that the three different powers in the state are "**first**, coordinate with one another as so many moral persons, that is, each complements the others to complete they constitution of a state." "But, **second**, they are also **subordinate** to one another, so that one of them, in assisting another, cannot also usurp its function; instead, each has its own principle" (DR, §48, 6:316). All three functions are necessary to complete the work of the state, as the analogy with the practical syllogism shows, and to ensure that distributive justice does result each of the functions has to be carried out by a separate

The Moral Foundation of Right   47

person, with none usurping the functions of one or both of the others.[71] Yet Kant is also emphatic that "The legislative power can belong only to the united will of the people," for only then can the principle *volenti non fit iniuria*, no wrong is done to those who are willing or consent, be satisfied,[72] while the executive is merely an *agent* of the legislative authority, even though the executive gets the name of the "ruler," for example, king or prince, of a state: "The **ruler** [*Regent*] of a state (*rex, princeps*) is that (moral or natural) person to whom the executive power (*potestas executioria*) belongs," *but* he is

> the agent [*Agent*] of the state, who appoints the magistrates and prescribes to the people rules in accordance with which each of them can acquire something or preserve what is his in conformity with the law. . . . His **orders** to the people, and to the magistrates and their superior (minister), who are obliged with the **administration of the state** (*gubernatio*), are ordinances or **decrees** (not laws); for they pertain to the decision in a particular case and are given as subject to change. (DR, §49, 6:316)

This suggests that while the executive is the agent of the legislature, the judiciary is in turn the agent of the executive, when one might have thought that both executive and judiciary should be considered as agents of the legislature, one charged with applying the laws that it has passed to particular cases and the other to enforcing those decisions (although Kant is prescient that the executive branch in a complex modern state also has a role in applying the law, namely, the rule-making function of executive agencies that transform the intent of the legislature into determinate rules). But what is particularly tricky is the relation between legislature and executive. On the one hand, Kant is clear that the law must express the united will of all who are subject to it, and a legislature is the instrument for the expression of that will.[73] He is likewise clear that the

---

[71] The distinction between three different *functions* or *powers* of government was a commonplace in Kant's time, certainly since Montesquieu's *Spirit of the Laws* (1748). Kant's argument that these three functions must be assigned to three different *persons* or branches was not. Its practice was embedded in the American constitutional system of "checks and balances"; Kant's position is a clear departure from Achenwall. See Guyer (2020a) and (2021).

[72] The idea of the "united will of the people" or a "general will" obviously has to be interpreted carefully. In a genuine republic, as opposed to one in name only, unanimity about any particular policy would be highly unusual, so majority or even plurality rule will have to do at that level. It is more reasonable to hope for unanimity about the constitution or basic law (*Grundgesetz*) of a state, although even that will no doubt require the imputation of tacit consent to many inhabitants.

[73] Kant assumes that the legislature will be an assembly of representatives or delegates elected by at least some of the citizenry, namely, "active citizens" who on account of their ownership of means of production (to use a later term) can be regarded as independent rather than as subject to the will of another, as are "passive citizens" such as women and those who work for wages. The argument for this distinction, not uncommon in Kant's time, was that dependents would have to vote as their masters wanted, and thus unfairly multiply the voting power of their masters. Needless to say, Kant's position on this does not conform to later assumptions about universal

executive must be charged merely with carrying out those laws, in that sense be the mere agent of the legislature, and his use of terms like "regent," "king," and "prince" might seem as if it just a sop to the pride of current kings, such as the king of Prussia, who might think that their role is greater than that. On the other hand, Kant is insistent that the executive must have a monopoly on the use of force, for it is the executive who is charged with the use of coercion to enforce the laws. Thus, the legislature may "take the ruler's authority away from him, depose him, or reform his administration" – "But it cannot **punish** him" (6:317) – for then there would be more than one coercive power within a state, and the result would be chaos, a return to the state of nature rather than a civil condition. (In American terms, Kant grants the legislature the political power of impeaching the executive, but not penal power over the executive, since punishment is the prerogative of the executive.)

This is the formal structure of republican government. Kant also addresses the matter of republican government, that is, the basic civil and political rights that such a government must make determinate and secure:

> The members of such a society who are united for giving law (*societas civilis*), that is, members of a state, are called **citizens of a state** (*cives*). In terms of rights, the attributes of a citizen, inseparable from his essence (as a citizen), are: lawful **freedom**, the attribute of obeying no other law than that to which he has given his consent;[74] civil **equality**, that of not recognizing among the **people** any superior with the moral capacity to bind him as a matter of right in a way that he could not in turn bind the other; and third, the attribute of civil **independence**, of owing his existence and preservation to his own rights and powers as a member of the commonwealth, not to the power of choice (*Willkühr*) of another among the people. (DR, §46, 6:314)

These civil rights restate the components of the innate right to freedom within the framework of public Right. By means of its tripartite structure, republican government is to make the innate Right to freedom determinate and secure, and since the right to acquire property under rightful conditions is also part of the innate Right to freedom, the role of government is also to make property rights determinate and secure. In John Locke's famous words, the purpose of government is to secure "Life, Health, Liberty, or Possessions";[75] in Kant's theory, it is to secure life and liberty, as the innate Right to freedom, and property as the result of the exercise of the right to acquire things which is itself part of innate Right. Kant's insistence upon the republican form of government is another manifestation of his moral foundation for the rule of law.

---

suffrage. For discussion, see Williams (1983, pp. 178–82); Pinkard (1999); Kersting (2004, pp. 131–4); and Hirsch (2017, pp. 328–34).

[74] See the previous note.   [75] Locke (1960, Second Treatise, chapter II, §6, p. 289).

The Moral Foundation of Right

Now comes a further argument for the moral foundation of legal and political rule. As already mentioned, Kant assumes that actual governments have arisen in situations of conflict and violence and that their rulers have typically not come to power through genuinely republican election by uncoerced electors – a fair enough assumption in eighteenth-century Europe, when even electoral kingship had long since given way to hereditary absolutism. He also holds that while rulers, that is, executives, can and should enforce the law by the threat and when necessary the exercise of coercion, they themselves cannot be coerced – otherwise there would be, again, chaos or anarchy, not government. But this means, to bring on stage one of Kant's most famous images, that while the crooked timber of the *subjects* of rulers can be made to grow straight by establishment and enforcement of the law, thus without need for the motivation of respect for the moral law itself, there is no one to exercise coercion against the rulers in a state – *yet they are made of the same crooked timber as everyone else*. As Kant puts it in the Sixth Proposition of his 1784 essay on the "Idea for a Universal History with a Cosmopolitan Aim," the ordinary

> human being **has need of a master**. For he certainly misuses his freedom in regard to others of his same kind; and although as a rational creature he wishes a law that sets limits to the freedom of all, his selfish animal inclination still misleads him into excepting itself from it where he may. . . . But where will he get this master? Nowhere else but from the human species. But then this master is exactly as much as an animal who has need of a master. . . . This problem is therefore the most difficult of all; indeed, its perfect solution is even impossible; out of such crooked timber as the human being is made, nothing entirely straight can be fabricated. (IUH, 8:23)

The problem is that anyone in a position of power is just as human as anyone else, therefore just as tempted to make exceptions to morality including justice in his own favor as anyone else is, and while subjects can nevertheless be induced to act within the law (at least for the most part) by the threat of punishment or actual punishment, those at the top of the system, with no one above them, cannot be coerced into rightful behavior, therefore into rightful administration of the whole system. And since justice can be secured only by the legislation and administration of just laws, injustice at the top can pervert the entire system. This problem will arise in an autocracy, of course, but it will also arise even in a formally constituted republic, where the three branches have the appropriate independence from each other, because there must be people at the highest level of each branch, thus members of the legislature and their leaders, the highest officer in the executive branch, the judges of the highest court in a judicial system, who have nobody above them to coerce them into rightful conduct, whether in legislation, adjudication, or enforcement. The problem is only exacerbated by the ascription of the sole power of coercion to the executive; and while a power of impeachment may nominally give superiority to the legislature over both executive and judiciary, it may be difficult to exercise and give the executive the upper hand in practice if not in theory.[76]

What is the solution to the problem of crooked timber? Although it offers only an approximation to a solution, Kant says it must be this: "correct concepts of the nature of a possible constitution, great experience practiced through many courses of life, and beyond this a good will that is prepared to accept it," although "three such items are very difficult to find altogether, and if it happens, it will only be very late," in the history of any state, or in human history altogether, "after many fruitless attempts" (8:23–4). Kant's use of the phrase "good will" in 1784 – as with the lectures on natural right, the very period in which he was composing the *Groundwork* – is a sure indicator that he regards rulers of any kind as having a moral obligation to conform their polities to the requirements of Right and through their use of their power to conform the behavior of those that they rule to the moral demands of Right. While external, aversive incentives can substitute for the internal motivation of respect for the moral law among the subjects, only their own ethical motivation can ensure that rulers will rule in a rightful fashion, and that makes sense only if the rule of Right is itself required by morality itself. In Kant's terminology, legality will suffice for subjects, but rulers must be moved by morality. Only their own morality can ensure that what is required for legality in their state is defined by morals.

A decade later Kant makes the same point in *Toward Perpetual Peace*. In this work, written in the form of a mock treaty, Kant outlines preliminary and definitive articles for the establishment of perpetual peace, which in the *Doctrine of Right* itself he characterizes as "the entire final end of the doctrine of Right within the limits of pure reason; for the condition of peace is alone that condition in which what is mine and what is yours for a multitude of human beings living in proximity to one another is secured under **laws**" (DR, Conclusion, 6:355). The preliminary articles are rules that must be followed during hostilities to make subsequent peace even possible, while the definitive articles are the rules that must be followed to establish such peace and make it enduring.[77] The former include such things as the abolition of standing armies and national debt for maintaining them, while the three definitive articles are that all states must become republics, republics must be associated in

---

[76] See Guyer (2021). For my previous discussions of the problem of the crooked timber of rulers, see Guyer (2009) and (2015).

[77] Ripstein (2021) discusses this contrast under the rubrics of "*Jus in bello*" (chapters 4–7) and "The Structure of Peace" (chapter 9).

a league of nations, and that states must receive visitors who wish to offer commerce in any form without hostility, although they need not enter into the proffered commerce or allow the visitors to immigrate.[78] Kant's basic idea is that in genuine republics where the citizens who would bear the costs of war without expecting any particular benefits from it have ultimate sovereignty there will be no will to make war, thus genuine republics would rather will that such conflicts as do inevitably arise, for example over boundaries, resources, or terms of trade, be peacefully arbitrated by an international organization, whose decisions they are committed to accept. These conditions are so obvious, Kant holds, that even a "nation of devils," that is, rational beings with understanding but driven only by self-love, can figure out the solution to the problem of peace, as if it were a mathematical problem (TPP, First Supplement, 8:366). However, the solution can be implemented only if all states *do* transform themselves into genuine republics, and for that it requires not devils but "moral politicians," who "will make it [their] principle that, once defects that could not have been prevented are found within the constitution of a state or in the relation of states, it is a duty, especially for heads of state, to be concerned about how they can be improved as soon as possible and brought into conformity with natural right, which stands before us as a model in the idea of reason." The key is that even though such rulers are not subject to coercion in the way that their subjects are, they are willing to bear "the cost of sacrifices to their self-seeking" (TPP, Appendix I, 8:372). Unlike the devils with theoretical but no pure practical reason, moral politicians can override self-interest out of sheer respect for the moral law. Again, this makes sense only if it is morality that requires the condition of Right in the first place.

Addressing himself as he is to an autocratic audience, the princes ruling the warring states of Europe (and by 1795, after the Terror, even France was a republic in name more than reality), Kant let them know that they are not expected to transform their principalities into republics overnight nor alone, thus that their subjects have a duty to undergo moral transformation as well:

> Since the severing of a bond of civil or cosmopolitan union even before a better constitution is ready to take its place is contrary to all political prudence, which agrees with morals in this, it would indeed be absurd to require that those defects be altered at once and violently, but it can be required of the one in power that he at least keep constantly approaching the end [*Zwecke*, i.e., goal] (of the best constitution in accordance with laws of right) ... until the people become susceptible to the influence of the idea of

---

[78] There has been a large debate about how comprehensive Kant's conception of "cosmopolitan law" should be; see especially Kleingeld (2012). Here I am staying with Kant's minimalistic conception of it.

the mere idea of the authority of the law (just as if it possessed physical power) and thus it is found fit to legislate for itself (such legislation being originally based on Right). (8:372)[79]

In the *Metaphysics of Morals*, as we saw, Kant maintains that the duties of Right *can* always be fulfilled ethically, that is, out of respect for the moral law itself, but that they never *have* to be. Here he seems to be suggesting that ultimately the members of a state *should* be motivated by respect for the moral law, but in any case he is also suggesting that *rulers* must go first, and that they can only be ethically motivated in so doing. Again, this makes sense only if it is morally incumbent upon them to realize Right.

Kant expresses his view of the moral obligation of politicians in the form of their obligation to transform their nonrepublican states into republics. But, of course, we know that any state regardless of its form can degenerate, and that republics have to be maintained even once they have been established. According to legend, Benjamin Franklin certainly knew that when, asked what sort of government the drafters of the Constitution had established, he replied "A republic, if you can keep it"; and those of us in the United States or elsewhere who are living through the Trump years know it too. Politicians who are in positions of power and who are as clever as they are self-interested can always pervert even the best-designed institutions. The obligation of politicians in power to respect the moral law and the duties of Right that arise from is unremitting even if in a state that is not merely well-designed but also well-run everyone else can be motivated by self-interest to do what morality requires. Politicians should always be moral politicians.

4.3 The Moral Obligation of Subjects

The moral foundation of Right is evident in Kant's argument about subjects rather than rulers: that they must have the right to inform their rulers of injustices and to petition for reform, but they do not have a right to rebel. Kant's argument is not merely that they cannot have a legal or constitutional right to rebel, but they do not have a moral right to rebel, for they have a moral obligation to remain in the civil condition once established.

Kant's argument against a right to rebellion proceeds in several steps. In the 1793 essay on "Theory and Practice," he starts by arguing that subjects do not

---

[79] Kant's view that even moral politicians cannot and should not try to implement their reforms overnight has led Christoph Horn to propose what he regards as an intermediate position in the debate about the independence thesis, a conception of "non-ideal normativity" that is neither pure morality nor pure prudence; see Horn (2014) and (2016). This does not seem right, since it will be either mere prudence or else morality itself which provides reasons for implementing change gradually.

have a right to rebel for the sake of what they expect will be their greater happiness, for the purpose of the state is not to secure their happiness in the first place, but to secure the rule of Right. Does the people have the right to resist a piece of legislation, Kant asks, that they view as "in all probability ... detrimental to their happiness"? No, because "what is under discussion here," that is, what is the proper function of the state, "is not the happiness that a subject may expect from the institution or administration of a commonwealth but above all merely the right that is to be secured for each by means of it, which is the supreme principle for which all maxims having to do with a commonwealth must proceed and which is limited by no other principle" (TP, 8:297–8). This already implies that the demand for Right is not a matter of prudence – but for Kant the only alternative is that it is a matter of morality. Kant anchors this argument in a ringing statement of the fundamental principle of his philosophy of Right:

> The saying *Salus publica supremacivitatis lex est* remains undiminished in its worth and authority; but the public well-being that must **first** be taken into account is precisely that lawful constitution which secures everyone his freedom by laws, whereby each remains at liberty to seek his happiness in whatever way seems best to him, provided he does not infringe upon that universal freedom in conformity with law and hence upon the right of other fellow citizens. (TP, 8:298)

The goal of morality in general is universal freedom in conformity with law, not happiness; the goal of government is securing universal freedom in conformity with law in our external relations with each other; so its failure in no other regard could provide a basis for resistance to it.

But what if what would move a populace to forcible resistance against their government is their judgment of its injustice, not their judgment of its imprudence? Surely people can be roused to rebellion by their sense of justice denied rather than self-interest impaired. Would not the failure of a government at its fundamental task be a good reason, indeed a moral reason, for resisting and if possible overthrowing that government? Kant has further arguments that do not turn on the claim that the happiness of the people is not the goal of government in the first place. One of these is what might be called a constitutional argument: a constitution cannot include a right on the part of the people – or, as is more likely, some self-appointed segment of the people – to resist or overthrow its designated supreme authority, which is or will include an executive with a monopoly on the use of coercion, because then that supreme authority will not be a supreme authority after all, and the constitution will be self-contradictory.

> The ground of this is that in an already existing civil constitution the people's judgment to determine how the constitution should be administered is no longer valid. For suppose that the people can so judge, and indeed contrary to the judgment of the actual head of state; who is to decide on which side the right is? Neither can make the decision as judge in his own suit. Hence there would have to be another head above the head of state, that would decide between him and the people; and this is self-contradictory. (TP, 8:301; cf. DR, General Remark A, 6:319–20)

"Indeed, even the constitution cannot contain any article that would make it possible for there to be some authority in a state to resist the supreme commander in case he should violate the law of the constitution," for in that case the "supreme commander in a state" would not be the supreme commander after all (6:319). It would be self-contradictory for a constitution to allow two supreme authorities, one appointed according to its procedures and the other by the people as such, self-appointed when they think that best, and while it might seem that this contradiction could be avoided by appointing yet another head over both, what is to prevent either the people or the now-supplanted ruler from rebelling against that head? Yet another really supreme authority? And then? The contradiction could be avoided only by an infinite regress – not much of an improvement. So again Kant concludes that "a people cannot offer any resistance to the legislative head of a state which would be consistent with Right" (DR, General Remark A, 6:319), where "the legislative head of a state" could mean either the legislature itself, on his account the true seat of sovereignty, or an executive appointed according to the rules set by the legislature and its agent. But apparently this is to hold even if the legislative and executive powers are combined in the hands of a single autocrat, although they should not be so combined in a proper republic. The only alternative is that the people have the right to petition for reforms, and that rulers have a moral duty to undertake necessary reforms – properly speaking an ethical duty, enforceable only by their own respect for the moral law. "A change in a (defective) constitution, which may certainly be necessary at times, can therefore be carried out only through **reform** by the sovereign itself, but not by the people, and therefore not by **revolution**" (6:321–2).

Kant goes even further and insists that

> A people should not **inquire** with any practical aim in view into the origin of the supreme authority to which it is subject ... For since a people must be regarded as already united under a general legislative will in order to judge with rightful force about the supreme authority (*summum imperium*), it cannot and may not judge otherwise than as the present head of state (*summus imperans*) wills it to ... the presently existing legislative authority ought to be obeyed, whatever its origin. (DR, General Remark A, 6:318–19)

Friedrich Bouterwek called this "the most paradoxical of all the paradoxical Kantian propositions ... that the mere **Idea** of overlordship [*Oberherrschaft*] should necessitate me to obey anyone who sets himself up as my lord [*Herr*] without asking who has given him the right to command me."[80] Bouterwek was the only reviewer of the book to whom Kant responded, in an Appendix added to the second edition of the *Rechtslehre*, but his response to this question was to argue that a people in "appearance" rather than as "thing in itself" is a people united by an actual constitution, warts and all, rather than by an ideal constitution, so that people must act in accordance with their actual constitution – thus "even though this constitution may be afflicted with great defects and gross faults and to be in need eventually of important improvements, it is still absolutely unpermitted and culpable to resist it," for again that "would result in a supreme will that destroys itself," a constitution that includes the contradiction that its designated supreme authority is not supreme after all (DR, Appendix, Conclusion, 6:371–2).

But something more than the threat of a formal violation of the law of noncontradiction in a right to rebellion bothered Kant. This is that rebellion, even if aimed solely at greater justice, could not actually happen without a reversion to the state of nature, that is to say, to anarchy, and thus represents a violation of our moral obligation to become and remain part of a civil condition. This real worry is expressed in a footnote in the essay on "Theory and Practice":

> Even if an actual contract of the people with the ruler has been violated, the people cannot react at once **as a commonwealth**[81] but only as a mob.[82] For the previously existing constitution has been torn up by the people, while their organization into a new commonwealth has not yet taken place. It is here that the condition of anarchy arises with all the horrors that are at least possible by means of it. (TP, 8:302 n)

This is what really moved Kant to reject a purported right to rebellion. No one actually thought that this could be a constitutional right, a right endorsed by a constitution, but defenders going back to John Locke thought that it was a moral right. But Kant thinks that it is morality itself that commands us to exit the state of nature and enter into the civil condition. So morality can never command us to revert to the state of nature.

The obvious objection to this is that some states are civil conditions in name only but in fact are nothing other than a war of some against others dressed up in

---

[80] Bouterwek (1797, p. 93; my translation).
[81] A *gemeines Wesen*, literally, a "common being."
[82] *durch Rottirung*, from the verb *rottieren*, to act like a criminal gang.

the trappings of law and legitimacy. Think of the Nazi "state," which, apart from its aggression on the other states of Europe, carried on war against Jews, Roma, homosexuals, and the mentally disabled, yet dressed itself up with courts and even with a legal theorist, Carl Schmitt, whom some who would be horrified to think of themselves as Nazis persist in taking seriously to this day. Or think of Stalin's show trials. It can be argued that some so-called states are not states at all, for quite apart from their formal organization they do not materially govern in the spirit of a Kantian republic, thus they have already dissolved any genuine state into an anarchical state of nature, and the opprobrium of doing that cannot be placed on the head of the people who would resist, for example the 1944 plotters against Hitler.[83] Whatever might be said in behalf of this position, Kant's response to Bouterwek makes it clear that Kant did not accept it: he recognized that actual states, states "in appearance," would not be perfectly just, but did not see this as a reason to revise his rejection of a right to rebellion under any circumstances.

Rather, we will conclude this section, and the whole argument of this Element, with Kant's own conclusion that the people have the morally grounded right to "freedom of the pen" and rulers have the ethical obligation to reform their states in the direction of genuine republics in both form and matter, that is, in their division of powers and their assurance of the basic rights due to their citizens simply in virtue of their humanity. As Kant writes in "Theory and Practice,"

> A nonrecalcitrant subject must be able to assume that his ruler does not **want** to do him wrong. Accordingly, <u>since every human being still has his inalienable rights</u>, which he can never give up even if he wanted to and about which he is authorized to judge for himself... a citizen must have, with the approval of the ruler himself, the authorization to make known publicly his opinions about what it is in the ruler's arrangements that seems to him to be a wrong against the commonwealth. For, to assume that the head of state could never err or be ignorant of something would be to represent him as favored with divine inspiration and raised above humanity. Thus **freedom of the pen** – kept within the limits of esteem and love for the constitution within which one lives by the subject's liberal way of thinking, which the constitution itself instills in them (and pens themselves also keep one another within these limits, so that they do not lose their freedom) – is the sole palladium of the people's rights. (TP, 8:304, underlining added)

---

[83] Those who have taken this line include Ripstein (2009, pp. 337–43), and Byrd and Hruschka (2010, pp. 181–4). Williams (1983, p. 201) recognizes that Kant did not allow for such a case. The most extensive discussion on Kant on the right to rebellion is in German, in Hirsch (2017, pp. 337–421).

But it *is* the palladium, that is, the knight champion, of the people's rights, and the people have a right to it, that is, the constitution of their state must include the freedom of the pen, and thus of the press (the only mass medium that Kant knew). This is the political realization of the right to freedom of speech that is part of the innate right to freedom. Thus freedom of the pen and the press is a moral right of human beings, and it is a moral obligation of rulers to concede it. Conversely, if rulers should be moral politicians, then it is a moral obligation for them to concede this right, and not just that, but also actually to reform the administration of their state – or, if legislators, the legislation of the state – to conform to the ideal of a rightful civil condition – in the terms of Kant's response to Friedrich Bouterwek, to bring the appearance of their states into better approximation of the state as thing in itself.

Abbreviations

CPrR = *Critique of Practical Reason* (in Kant 1996a)
CPR = *Critique of Pure Reason* (Kant 1998)
DR = *Doctrine of Right*, Part I of the *Metaphysics of Morals* (in Kant 1996a)
DV = *Doctrine of Virtue*, Part II of the *Metaphysics of Morals* (in Kant 1996a)
G = *Groundwork for the Metaphysics of Morals* (in Kant 1996a)
IUH = "Idea for a Universal History" (in Kant 2007)
Eth-K = *Lectures on Moral Philosophy* (*Vorlesungen zur Moralphilosophie*)
L-NR = *Lectures on Naturrecht/Feyerabend*
MMI = *Metaphysics of Morals*, Introduction (in Kant 1996a)
R = *Reflexionen* (entries in Kant's *handschriftliche Nachlaß*, i.e., surviving notes)
Rel = *Religion within the Boundaries of Mere Reason* (in Kant 1996b)
ROFBS = *Remarks in the Observations on the Feeling of the Beautiful and Sublime* (in Kant 2011)
TP = "On the Common Saying: That May Be Correct in Theory, but It Is of No Use in Practice" (in Kant 1996a)
TPP = *Towards Perpetual Peace* (in Kant 1996a)

References

Kant's Works

Kant, Immanuel, 1887. *The Philosophy of Law*. Translated by W. Hastie. Clifton: August M. Kelley.

Kant, Immanuel, 1900–. *Kant's gesammelte Schriften*. Edited by the Royal Prussian, subsequently German, then Berlin-Brandenburg, Academy of Sciences. 29 vols. Berlin: Georg Reimer, subsequently Walter de Gruyter.

Kant, Immanuel, 1986. *Metaphysische Anfangsgründe der Rechtslehre: Philosophische Bibliothek 360*. Edited by Bernd Ludwig. Hamburg: Felix Meiner Verlag.

Kant, Immanuel, 1992. *Theoretical Philosophy 1775–1770*. Edited and translated by David Walford in collaboration with Ralf Meerbote. Cambridge: Cambridge University Press.

Kant, Immanuel, 1996a. *Practical Philosophy*. Edited and translated by Mary J. Gregor. Cambridge: Cambridge University Press.

Kant, Immanuel, 1996b. *Religion and Rational Theology*. Edited and translated by Allen W. Wood and George di Giovanni. Cambridge: Cambridge University Press.

Kant, Immanuel, 1997. *Lectures on Ethics*. Edited by Peter Heath and J. B. Schneewind, translated by Peter Heath. Cambridge: Cambridge University Press.

Kant, Immanuel, 1998. *Critique of Pure Reason*. Edited and translated by Paul Guyer and Allen W. Wood. Cambridge: Cambridge University Press.

Kant, Immanuel, 1999. *Metaphysical Elements of Justice*. Translated by John Ladd, Second edition. Indianapolis: Hackett.

Kant, Immanuel, 2004. *Vorlesungen zur Moralphilosophie*. Edited by Werner Stark and Manfred Kuehn. Berlin: Walter de Gruyter.

Kant, Immanuel, 2005. *Notes and Fragments*. Edited by Paul Guyer, translated by Curtis Bowman, Paul Guyer, and Frederick Rauscher. Cambridge: Cambridge University Press.

Kant, Immanuel, 2007. *Anthropology, History, and Education*. Edited by Robert B. Louden and Günter Zöller. Cambridge: Cambridge University Press.

Kant, Immanuel, 2010–14. *Kant-Index Band 30: Stellenindex und Konkordanz zum "Naturrecht Feyerabend."* Edited by Heinrich P. Delfosse, Norbert Hinske, and Gianluca Sadun Bordoni. 3 vols. Stuttgart-Bad Canstatt: Frommann-Holzboog.

Kant, Immanuel, 2011. *Observations on the Feeling of the Beautiful and Sublime and Other Writings*. Edited by Patrick Frierson and Paul Guyer. Cambridge: Cambridge University Press.

Kant, Immanuel, 2016. *Lectures and Drafts on Political Philosophy.* Edited by Frederick Rauscher, translated by Frederick Rauscher and Kenneth R. Westphal. Cambridge: Cambridge University Press.

Other References

Achenwall, Gottfried, 2020a. *Natural Law.* Edited by Pauline Kleingeld, translated by Corinna Vermeulen, with an Introduction by Paul Guyer. London: Bloomsbury.

Achenwall, Gottfried, 2020b. *Prolegomena to Natural Law.* Edited by Pauline Kleingeld, translated by Corinna Vermeulen. Groningen: University of Groningen Press.

Achenwall, Gottfried, and Johann Stephan Pütter, 1995. *Anfangsgründe des Naturrechts (Elementa Iuris Naturae).* Edited and translated by Jan Schröder. Frankfurt am Main: Insel Verlag.

Allison, Henry E., 1973. *The Kant-Eberhard Controversy.* Baltimore: The Johns Hopkins University Press.

Allison, Henry E., 2004. *Kant's Transcendental Idealism: An Interpretation and Defense.* Revised edition (originally 1983). New Haven: Yale University Press.

Allison, Henry E., 2011. *Kant's Groundwork for the Metaphysics of Morals: A Commentary.* Oxford: Oxford University Press.

Baiasu, Sorin, 2016. "Right's Complex Relation to Ethics in Kant: The Limits of Independentism." *Kant-Studien* 107: 2–33.

Baumgarten, Alexander Gottlieb, 2020. *Baumgarten's Elements of First Practical Philosophy: A Critical Translation with Kant's Reflections on Moral Philosophy.* Edited and translated by Courtney D. Fugate and John Hymers. London: Bloomsbury.

Beck, Lewis White, 1965. "Can Kant's Synthetic Judgments Be Made Analytic?" *Kant-Studien* 68 (1955): 168–81, reprinted in Beck, *Studies in the Philosophy of Kant.* Indianapolis: Bobbs-Merrill, pp. 74–98.

Beiser, Frederick C., 1992. *Enlightenment, Revolution, and Romanticism: The Genesis of Modern German Political Thought, 1790–1800.* Cambridge, Mass.: Harvard University Press.

Bouterwek, Friedrich, 1797. Review of *Metaphysische Anfangsgründe der Naturrecht, Göttingische Anzeigen von gelehrten Sachen*, pp. 265–76, reprinted in Klippel, Hüning, and Eisfeld 2021, pp. 87–93.

Byrd, B. Sharon, and Joachim Hruschka, 2010. *Kant's Doctrine of Right: A Commentary.* Cambridge: Cambridge University Press.

Carl, Wolfgang, 1989. *Der schweigende Kant: Die Entwürfe zu einer Deduktion der Kategorien vor 1781.* Göttingen: Vandenhoeck & Ruprecht.

References

Dean, Richard, 2006. *The Value of Humanity in Kant's Moral Theory*. Oxford: Oxford University Press.

Gregor, Mary J., 1963. *Laws of Freedom: A Study of Kant's Method of Applying the Categorical Imperative in the* Metaphysik der Sitten. Oxford: Basil Blackwell.

Guyer, Paul, 1987. *Kant and the Claims of Knowledge*. Cambridge: Cambridge University Press.

Guyer, Paul, 2000. *Kant on Freedom, Law, and Happiness*. Cambridge: Cambridge University Press.

Guyer, Paul, 2002. "Kant's Deductions of the Principles of Right." In Timmons 2002, pp. 24–64. Reprinted in Guyer, *Kant's System of Nature and Freedom: Selected Essays*. Oxford: Oxford University Press, 2005, pp. 198–242.

Guyer, Paul, 2009. "The Crooked Timber of Humankind." In *Kant's "Idea for a Universal History with a Cosmopolitan Aim": A Critical Guide*, edited by Amelie Rorty and James Schmidt. Cambridge: Cambridge University Press, pp. 129–49.

Guyer, Paul, 2010. "The Obligation to Be Virtuous: Kant's Conception of the *Tugendverpflichtung*." *Social Philosophy and Policy* 27: 306–32, reprinted in Guyer 2016a, pp. 216–34.

Guyer, Paul, 2012. "'Hobbes Is of the Opposite Opinion': Kant and Hobbes on the Three Authorities in the State." *Hobbes Studies* 25: 91–119.

Guyer, Paul, 2014. *Kant*. Second edition. London: Routledge.

Guyer, Paul, 2015. "Kant and the Moral Politicians." In *Scientific Statesmanship, Governance, and the History of Political Philosophy*, edited by Kyriakos N. Demetriou and Antis Loizides. London: Routledge, pp. 116–36.

Guyer, Paul, 2016a. *Virtues of Freedom: Selected Essays on Kant*. Oxford: Oxford University Press.

Guyer, Paul, 2016b. "The Twofold Morality of *Recht*: Once More unto the Breach." *Kant-Studien* 107: 34–63.

Guyer, Paul, 2017. "Transcendental Idealism: What and Why?" In *The Palgrave Kant Handbook*, edited by Matthew C. Altman. London: Palgrave Macmillan, pp. 71–90.

Guyer, Paul, 2019. *Kant on the Rationality of Morality*. Cambridge: Cambridge University Press.

Guyer, Paul, 2020a. "Achenwall, Kant, and the Division of Governmental Powers." In Ruffing, Schlitte, and Sadun Bordoni 2020, pp. 201–28.

Guyer, Paul, 2020b. "Mendelssohn, Kant, and Religious Pluralism." *Zeitschrift für philosophische Forschung* 68: 589–610.

Guyer, Paul, 2021. "Is Sovereignty Divided Still Sovereignty? Kant and *The Federalist*." *University of Pittsburgh Law Review* 83 (2021): 365–96.

Guyer, Paul, 2022a. "The Empire of Ends." *Proceedings and Addresses of the American Philosophical Association* 96: 204–37.

Guyer, Paul, 2022b. "Arguing for Freedom of Religion." *Roczniki Filozoficzne* 70: 365–94.

Guyer, Paul, forthcoming. "Enforcing the Law of Nature: The Background to Kant's Conception of the Relation between Morality and Recht." In *Kantian Citizenship: Grounds, Standards and Global Implications*, edited by Mark Timmons and Sorin Baisu. London: Routledge.

Herman, Barbara, 2021. *The Moral Habitat*. Oxford: Oxford University Press.

Hirsch, Philipp-Alexander, 2017. *Freiheit und Staatlichkeit bei Kant: Kant-Studien Ergänzungshefte* 194. Berlin: Walter de Gruyter.

Hobbes, Thomas, 2012. *Leviathan*. Edited by Noel Malcolm. 3 vols. Oxford: Clarendon Press.

Höffe, Otfried, 1990. *Kategorische Rechtsprinzipien: Ein Kontrapunkte der Moderne*. Frankfurt am Main: Suhrkamp.

Höffe, Otfried, 2002. *Categorical Principles of Law: A Counterpoint to Modernity*. Translated by Mark Migotti, Introduction by Kenneth Baynes. University Park: The Pennsylvania State University Press.

Höffe, Otfried, 2004. *Categorical Principles of Law: A Counterpoint to Modernity*. Translated by Mark Migotti. University Park: The Pennsylvania State University Press.

Horn, Christoph, 2014. *Nichtideale Normativität: Ein neuer Blick auf Kants politische Philosophie*. Frankfurt am Main: Suhrkamp Verlag.

Horn, Christoph, 2016. "Kant's Political Philosophy as a Theory of Non-ideal Normativity." *Kant-Studien* 107: 89–110.

Jakob, Ludwig Heinrich, 1797. Review of Kant's *Rechtslehre*, in *Annalen der Philosophie und des philosophischen Geistes von einer Gesellschaft gelehter Männer*, vol. 3 (Leipzig: Kleefeld, 1797), columns 13–58, reprinted in Klippel, Hüning, and Eisfeld 2021, pp. 50–76.

Johnson, Robert N., 1996. "Kant's Conception of Merit." *Pacific Philosophical Quarterly* 77: 310–34.

Kersting, Wolfgang, 2004. *Kant über Recht*. Paderborn: Mentis.

Kleingeld, Pauline, 2012. *Kant and Cosmopolitanism: The Philosophical Ideal of World Citizenship*. Cambridge: Cambridge University Press.

Klemme, Heiner F., 2023. *Die Selbsterhaltung der Vernunft: Kant und die Modernität seines Denkens*. Frankfurt am Main: Vittorio Klostermann.

Klippel, Diethelm, Dieter Hüning, and Jens Eisfeld, editors, 2021. *Die Rezensionen zu Kants Metaphysischen Anfangsgründe der Rechtslehre: Die zeitgenössische Rezeption von Kants Rechtsphilosophie*, Kant-Studien Ergänzungshefte 212. Berlin: Walter de Gruyter.

Korsgaard, Christine M., 1996. "Kant's Formula of Universal Law." *Pacific Philosophical Quarterly* 66 (1985): 24–47. Reprinted in Korsgaard, *Creating the Kingdom of Ends*. Cambridge: Cambridge University Press, pp. 77–105.

Korsgaard, Christine M., 2009. *Self-Constitution: Agency, Identity, and Integrity*. Oxford: Oxford University Press.

Locke, John, 1960. *Two Treatises of Government*. Edited by Peter Laslett. Cambridge: Cambridge University Press.

McCarty, Richard, 2009. *Kant's Theory of Action*. Oxford: Oxford University Press.

Mendelssohn, Moses, 2011. *Morning Hours: Lectures on God's Existence*. Translated by Daniel O. Dahlstrom and Corey Dyck. Dordrecht: Springer.

Mendelssohn, Moses, 2012. *Last Works*. Translated by Bruce Rosenstock. Urbana: University of Illinois Press.

Mill, John Stuart, 1977. *On Liberty* (1859). In *Collected Works of John Stuart Mill*, vol. XVIII, *Essays on Politics and Society*, Part I, edited by J. M. Robson. Toronto: University of Toronto Press, pp. 213–310.

Mulholland, Leslie A., 1990. *Kant's System of Rights*. New York: Columbia University Press.

Nance, Michael, 2012. "Kantian Right and the Categorical Imperative: Response to Willaschek." *International Journal of Philosophical Studies* 20: 541–56.

O'Neill, Onora, 2013. *Acting on Principle: An Essay on Kantian Ethics*. Second edition (originally 1975). Cambridge: Cambridge University Press.

Pauer-Studer, Herlinde, 2016. "'A Community of Ends': Kant's Realm of Ends and the Distinction between Internal and External Freedom." *Kant-Studien* 107: 125–59.

Pinkard, Terry, 1999. "Kant, Citizenship, and Freedom." In *Immanuel Kant: Metaphysische Anfangsgründe der Rechtslehre*, edited by Otfried Höffe. Berlin: Akademie Verlag, pp. 155–72.

Pinzani, Alessandro, 2021. "Wie kann Freiheit ein angeborenes Recht sein?" In *Zwischen Recht und Pflichten – Kant's "Metaphysik der Sitten,"* edited by Jean-Christophe Merle and Carola Freiin von Villiez. Berlin: Walter de Gruyter, pp. 79–94.

Pogge, Thomas, 2002. "Is Kant's *Rechtslehre* a 'Comprehensive Liberalism'?" In *Kant's Metaphysics of Morals: Interpretative Essays*, edited by Mark Timmons. Oxford: Oxford University Press, pp. 133–58.

Pufendorf, Samuel, 2003. *The Whole Duty of Man, according to the Law of Nature*. Translated by Andrew Tooke (1691), edited by Ian Hunter and David Saunders. Indianapolis: Liberty Fund.

Quine, Willard Van Orman, 1953. *From a Logical Point of View*. Cambridge, Mass.: Harvard University Press.

Rawls, John, 1989. "Themes from Kant." In Eckhart Förster, edited by *Kant's Transcendental Deductions: The Three Critiques and the Opus Postumum*. Stanford: Stanford University Press, pp. 81–113. Reprinted in Rawls, *Collected Papers*, edited by Samuel Freeman. Cambridge, Mass.: Harvard University Press, 1999, pp. 497–528.

Rawls, John, 1999. *A Theory of Justice*. Second edition (originally 1971). Cambridge, Mass.: Harvard University Press.

Rawls, John, 2000. *Lectures on the History of Moral Philosophy*. Edited by Barbara Herman. Cambridge, Mass.: Harvard University Press.

Rawls, John, 2001. *Justice as Fairness: A Restatement*. Edited by Erin Kelly. Cambridge, Mass.: Harvard University Press.

Rawls, John, 2005. *Political Liberalism*. Second edition (originally 1993). New York: Columbia University Press.

Ripstein, Arthur, 2009. *Force and Freedom: Kant's Legal and Political Philosophy*. Cambridge, Mass.: Harvard University Press.

Ripstein, Arthur, 2021. *Kant and the Law of War*. New York: Oxford University Press.

Rossi, Philip J., 2005. *The Social Authority of Reason: Kant's Critique, Radical Evil, and the Destiny of Humankind*. Albany: State University of New York Press.

Ruffing, Margit, Annika Schlitte, and Gianluca Sadun Bordoni, editors, 2020. *Kants Naturrecht Feyerabend: Analysen und Perspektiven*. Berlin: Walter de Gruyter.

Thomasius, Christian, 2011. *Institutes of Divine Jurisprudence, with Selections from Foundations of the Law of Nature and Nations*. Edited and translated by Thomas Ahnert. Indianapolis: Liberty Fund.

Timmermann, Jens, 2007. *Kant's Groundwork of the Metaphysics of Morals: A Commentary*. Cambridge: Cambridge University Press.

Timmermann, Jens, 2022. *Kant's Will at the Crossroads: An Essay on the Failings of Practical Rationality*. Oxford: Oxford University Press.

Timmons, Mark, editor, 2002. *Kant's Metaphysics of Morals: Interpretative Essays*. Oxford: Oxford University Press.

Werkmeister, William H., 1979. *Kant's Silent Decade: A Decade of Philosophical Development*. Tallahassee: University Presses of Florida.

Willaschek, Marcus, 1997. "Why the *Doctrine of Right* Does Not Belong in the *Metaphysics of Morals*: On Some Basic Distinctions in Kant's Moral Philosophy." *Jahrbuch für Recht und Ethik/Annual Review of Law and Ethics* 5: 205–27.

Willaschek, Marcus, 2002. "Which Imperatives for Right? On the Non-prescriptive Character of Juridical Laws in Kant's *Metaphysics of Morals*." In Timmons 2016, pp. 65–88.

References

Willaschek, Marcus, 2009. "Right and Coercion: Can Kant's Conception of Right Be Derived from His Moral Theory?" *International Journal of Philosophical Studies* 1: 49–70.

Williams, Howard, 1983. *Kant's Political Philosophy.* New York: St. Martin's.

Williams, Howard, 2003. *Kant's Critique of Hobbes.* Cardiff: University of Wales Press.

Wood, Allen W., 1999. *Kant's Ethical Thought.* Cambridge: Cambridge University Press.

Wood, Allen W, 2002. "The Final Form of Kant's Practical Philosophy." In Timmons 2002, pp. 1–22.

Wood, Allen W., 2008. *Kantian Ethics.* Cambridge: Cambridge University Press.

Wood, Allen W., 2014. *The Free Development of Each: Studies on Freedom, Right, and Ethics in Classical German Philosophy.* Oxford: Oxford University Press.

Zöller, Günter, 2020. "'Right Rests Solely on Freedom' (AA 27.2, 1336): The Historical and Systematic Significance of Kant's *Natural Law Feyerabend*." In Ruffing, Schlitte, and Sadun Bordoni 2020, pp. 33–50.

Cambridge Elements =

The Philosophy of Immanuel Kant

Desmond Hogan
Princeton University

Desmond Hogan joined the philosophy department at Princeton in 2004. His interests include Kant, Leibniz and German rationalism, early modern philosophy, and questions about causation and freedom. Recent work includes 'Kant on the Foreknowledge of Contingent Truths', *Res Philosophica* 91 (1) (2014); 'Kant's Theory of Divine and Secondary Causation', in Brandon Look (ed.) *Leibniz and Kant*, Oxford University Press (2021); 'Kant and the Character of Mathematical Inference', in Carl Posy and Ofra Rechter (eds.) *Kant's Philosophy of Mathematics Vol. I*, Cambridge University Press (2020).

Howard Williams
University of Cardiff

Howard Williams was appointed Honorary Distinguished Professor at the Department of Politics and International Relations, University of Cardiff in 2014. He is also Emeritus Professor in Political Theory at the Department of International Politics, Aberystwyth University, a member of the Coleg Cymraeg Cenedlaethol (Welsh-language national college) and a Fellow of the Learned Society of Wales. He is the author of *Marx* (1980); *Kant's Political Philosophy* (1983); *Concepts of Ideology* (1988); *Hegel, Heraclitus and Marx's Dialectic* (1989); *International Relations in Political Theory* (1992); *International Relations and the Limits of Political Theory* (1996); *Kant's Critique of Hobbes: Sovereignty and Cosmopolitanism* (2003); *Kant and the End of War* (2012) and is currently editor of the journal Kantian Review. He is writing a book on the Kantian legacy in political philosophy for a new series edited by Paul Guyer.

Allen Wood
Indiana University

Allen Wood is Ward W. and Priscilla B. Woods Professor Emeritus at Stanford University. He was a John S. Guggenheim Fellow at the Free University in Berlin, a National Endowment for the Humanities Fellow at the University of Bonn and Isaiah Berlin Visiting Professor at the University of Oxford. He is on the editorial board of eight philosophy journals, five book series and The Stanford Encyclopedia of Philosophy. Along with Paul Guyer, Professor Wood is co-editor of The Cambridge Edition of the Works of Immanuel Kant and translator of the Critique of Pure Reason. He is the author or editor of a number of other works, mainly on Kant, Hegel, and Karl Marx. His most recently published books are *Fichte's Ethical Thought*, Oxford University Press (2016) and *Kant and Religion*, Cambridge University Press (2020). Wood is a member of the American Academy of Arts and Sciences.

About the Series

This Cambridge Elements series provides an extensive overview of Kant's philosophy and its impact upon philosophy and philosophers. Distinguished Kant specialists provide an up-to-date summary of the results of current research in their fields and give their own take on what they believe are the most significant debates influencing research, drawing original conclusions.

Cambridge Elements

The Philosophy of Immanuel Kant

Elements in the Series

Kant and Global Distributive Justice
Sylvie Loriaux

Anthropology from a Kantian Point of View
Robert B. Louden

Introducing Kant's Critique of Pure Reason
Paul Guyer and Allen Wood

Kant's Theory of Conscience
Samuel Kahn

Rationalizing (Vernünfteln)
Martin Sticker

Kant and the French Revolution
Reidar Maliks

The Kantian Federation
Luigi Caranti

The Politics of Beauty: A Study of Kant's Critique of Taste
Susan Meld Shell

Kant's Theory of Labour
Jordan Pascoe

Kant's Late Philosophy of Nature: The Opus postumum
Stephen Howard

Kant on Freedom
Owen Ware

The Moral Foundation of Right
Paul Guyer

A full series listing is available at: www.cambridge.org/EPIK

Printed in the United States
by Baker & Taylor Publisher Services